Magical Spell Templates

Magical Spell Templates

Artwork & Design: Lazaros Georgoulas — lazageo@gmail.com

Printed by Createspace, An Amazon.com company.

ISBN-13: 978-1523281770
ISBN-10: 1523281774

Spell #: _____

Spell Name: _____

_____

Spell Items: _____ _____

_____ _____

_____ _____

_____ _____

_____ _____

Preferred Moon Phase: _____

Preferred Times of Day: 06:00 07:00 08:00 09:00
10:00 11:00 12:00 13:00 14:00 15:00 16:00 17:00
18:00 19:00 20:00 21:00 22:00 23:00 24:00 _____

_____

Spell Casting Details: _____

_____

_____

_____

_____

_____

_____

_____

_____

_____

_____

Spell #: _____

Spell Name: _____

_____

Spell Items: _____ _____

_____ _____

_____ _____

_____ _____

Preferred Moon Phase: _____

Preferred Times of Day: 06:00 07:00 08:00 09:00
10:00 11:00 12:00 13:00 14:00 15:00 16:00 17:00
18:00 19:00 20:00 21:00 22:00 23:00 24:00 _____

_____

Spell Casting Details: _____

_____

_____

_____

_____

_____

_____

_____

_____

_____

Spell #: _____

Spell Name: _____

_____

Spell Items: _____ _____

_____ _____ _____

_____ _____ _____

_____ _____ _____

_____ _____ _____

Preferred Moon Phase: _____

Preferred Times of Day: 06:00 07:00 08:00 09:00
10:00 11:00 12:00 13:00 14:00 15:00 16:00 17:00
18:00 19:00 20:00 21:00 22:00 23:00 24:00 _____

Spell Casting Details: _____

_____

_____

_____

_____

_____

_____

_____

_____

_____

Spell #: _____

Spell Name: _____

_____

Spell Items: _____ _____

_____ _____ _____

_____ _____ _____

_____ _____ _____

_____ _____ _____

Preferred Moon Phase: _____

Preferred Times of Day: 06:00 07:00 08:00 09:00
10:00 11:00 12:00 13:00 14:00 15:00 16:00 17:00
18:00 19:00 20:00 21:00 22:00 23:00 24:00 _____

Spell Casting Details: _____

_____

_____

_____

_____

_____

_____

_____

_____

_____

Spell #: _____

Spell Name: _____
_____

Spell Items: _____   _____
_____   _____   _____
_____   _____   _____
_____   _____   _____
_____   _____   _____

Preferred Moon Phase: _____

Preferred Times of Day: 06:00 07:00 08:00 09:00
10:00 11:00 12:00 13:00 14:00 15:00 16:00 17:00
18:00 19:00 20:00 21:00 22:00 23:00 24:00 _____

Spell Casting Details: _____
_____
_____
_____
_____
_____
_____
_____
_____
_____
_____

Spell #: _____

Spell Name: _____
_____

Spell Items: _____ _____
_____ _____ _____
_____ _____ _____
_____ _____ _____
_____ _____ _____

Preferred Moon Phase: _____

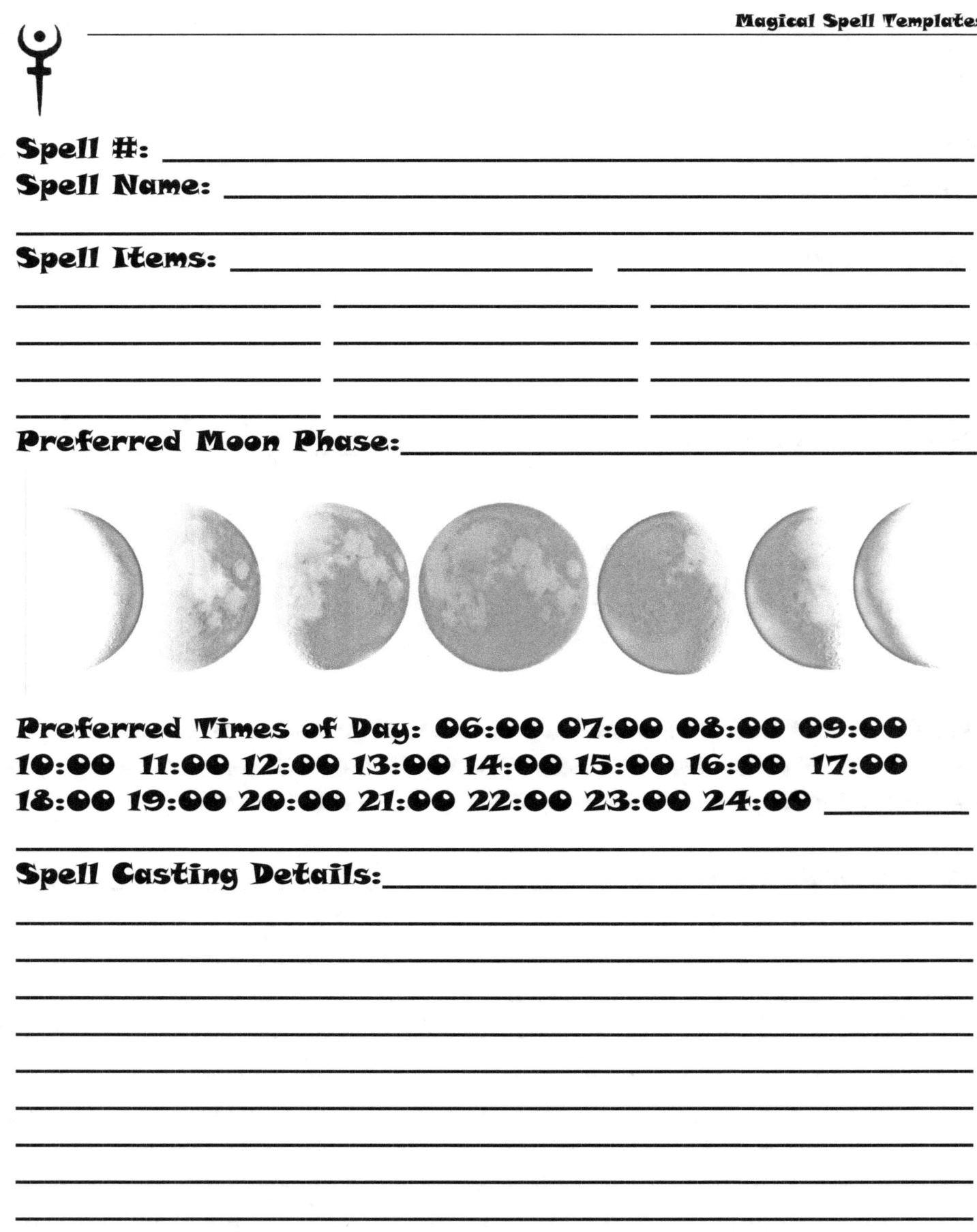

**Preferred Times of Day: 06:00 07:00 08:00 09:00
10:00 11:00 12:00 13:00 14:00 15:00 16:00 17:00
18:00 19:00 20:00 21:00 22:00 23:00 24:00 _____**
_____

Spell Casting Details: _____
_____
_____
_____
_____
_____
_____
_____
_____
_____
_____

Spell #: _____

Spell Name: _____

_____

Spell Items: _____ _____

_____ _____ _____

_____ _____ _____

_____ _____ _____

_____ _____ _____

Preferred Moon Phase: _____

Preferred Times of Day: 06:00 07:00 08:00 09:00
10:00 11:00 12:00 13:00 14:00 15:00 16:00 17:00
18:00 19:00 20:00 21:00 22:00 23:00 24:00 _____
_____

Spell Casting Details:_____

_____

_____

_____

_____

_____

_____

_____

_____

_____

_____

_____

Spell #: _____

Spell Name: _____

Spell Items: _____ _____

_____ _____

_____ _____

_____ _____

_____ _____

Preferred Moon Phase:_____

Preferred Times of Day: 06:00 07:00 08:00 09:00
10:00 11:00 12:00 13:00 14:00 15:00 16:00 17:00
18:00 19:00 20:00 21:00 22:00 23:00 24:00 _____

Spell Casting Details:_____

_____

_____

_____

_____

_____

_____

_____

_____

_____

Spell #: _____

Spell Name: _____

_____

Spell Items: _____ _____

_____ _____

_____ _____

_____ _____

_____ _____

Preferred Moon Phase: _____

Preferred Times of Day: 06:00 07:00 08:00 09:00
10:00 11:00 12:00 13:00 14:00 15:00 16:00 17:00
18:00 19:00 20:00 21:00 22:00 23:00 24:00 _____

Spell Casting Details: _____

_____

_____

_____

_____

_____

_____

_____

_____

_____

_____

Spell #: _____

Spell Name: _____

_____

Spell Items: _____   _____

_____   _____   _____

_____   _____   _____

_____   _____   _____

_____   _____   _____

Preferred Moon Phase: _____

**Preferred Times of Day: 06:00 07:00 08:00 09:00
10:00 11:00 12:00 13:00 14:00 15:00 16:00 17:00
18:00 19:00 20:00 21:00 22:00 23:00 24:00** _____

_____

Spell Casting Details: _____

_____

_____

_____

_____

_____

_____

_____

_____

_____

Spell #: _____

Spell Name: _____
_____

Spell Items: _____ _____
_____ _____ _____
_____ _____ _____
_____ _____ _____
_____ _____ _____

Preferred Moon Phase: _____

Preferred Times of Day: 06:00 07:00 08:00 09:00
10:00 11:00 12:00 13:00 14:00 15:00 16:00 17:00
18:00 19:00 20:00 21:00 22:00 23:00 24:00 _____

Spell Casting Details: _____
_____
_____
_____
_____
_____
_____
_____
_____
_____
_____

Spell #: _____

Spell Name: _____

_____

Spell Items: _____ _____

_____ _____ _____

_____ _____ _____

_____ _____ _____

_____ _____ _____

Preferred Moon Phase: _____

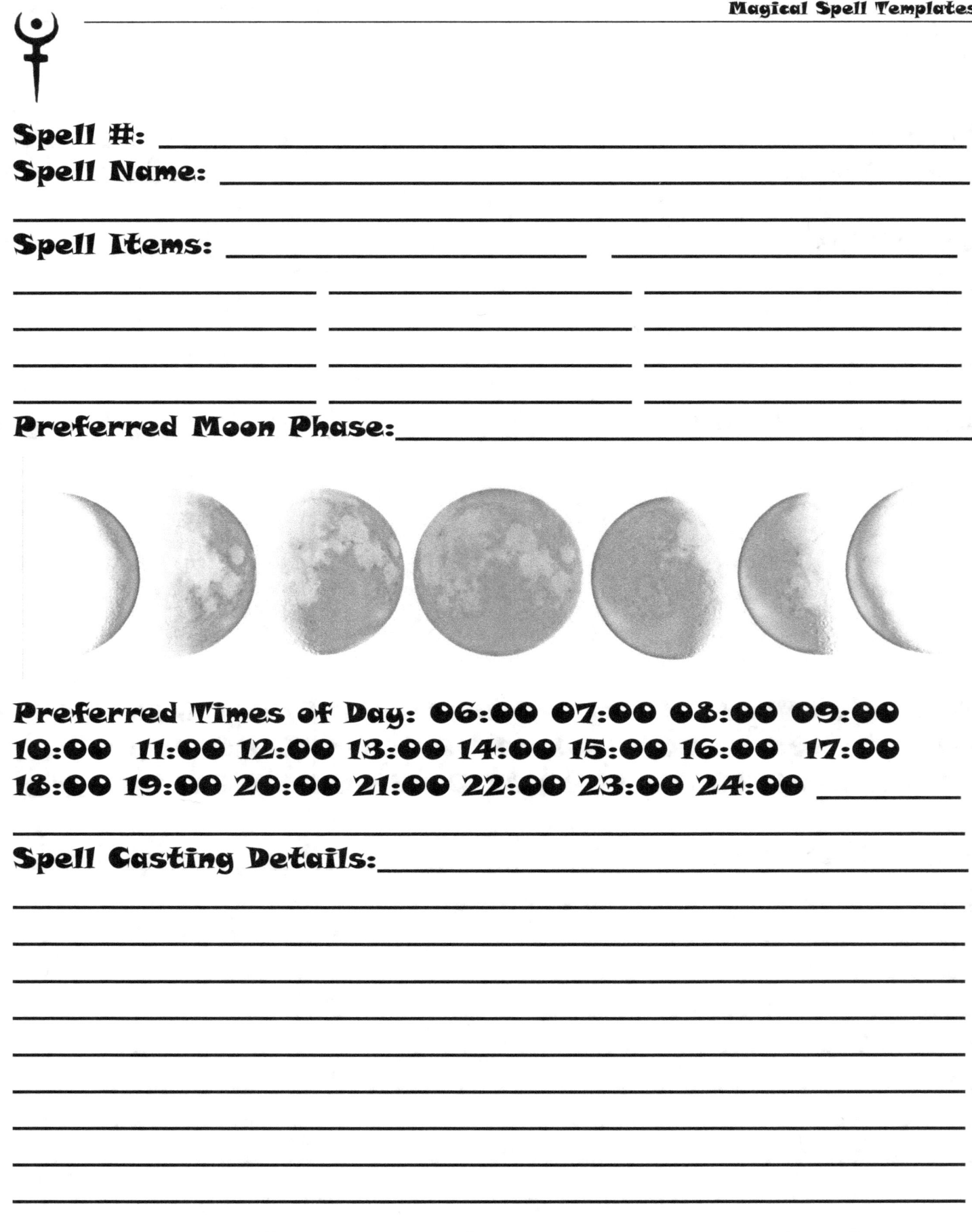

Preferred Times of Day: **06:00 07:00 08:00 09:00**
10:00 11:00 12:00 13:00 14:00 15:00 16:00 17:00
18:00 19:00 20:00 21:00 22:00 23:00 24:00 _____

_____

Spell Casting Details: _____

_____

_____

_____

_____

_____

_____

_____

_____

_____

Spell #: _____

Spell Name: _____

_____

Spell Items: _____ _____

_____ _____ _____

_____ _____ _____

_____ _____ _____

_____ _____ _____

Preferred Moon Phase: _____

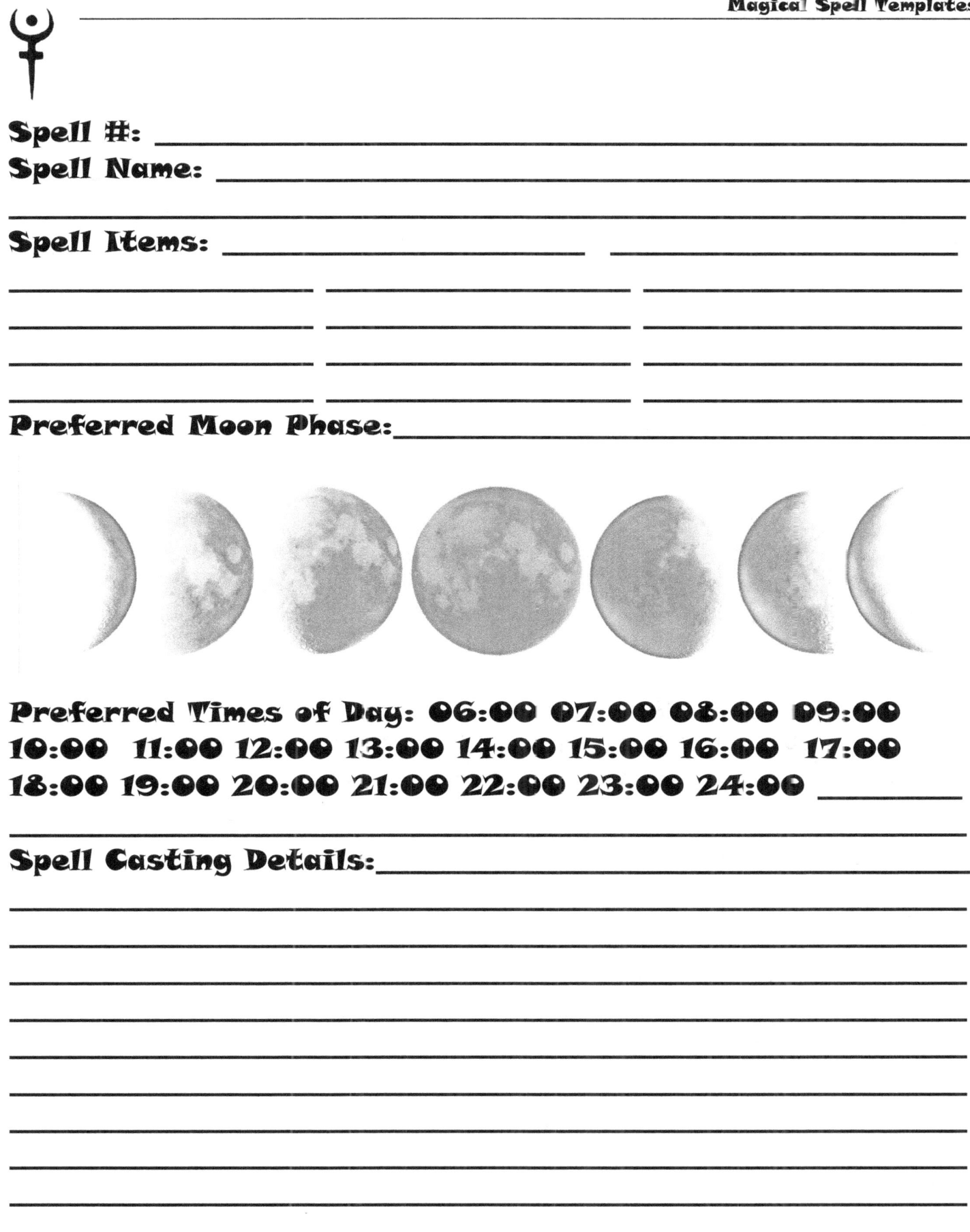

**Preferred Times of Day: 06:00 07:00 08:00 09:00
10:00   11:00 12:00 13:00 14:00 15:00 16:00   17:00
18:00 19:00 20:00 21:00 22:00 23:00 24:00** _____

_____

Spell Casting Details: _____

_____

_____

_____

_____

_____

_____

_____

_____

_____

_____

_____

Spell #: _____

Spell Name: _____
_____

Spell Items: _____ _____
_____ _____ _____
_____ _____ _____
_____ _____ _____
_____ _____ _____

Preferred Moon Phase: _____
_____

**Preferred Times of Day: 06:00 07:00 08:00 09:00
10:00 11:00 12:00 13:00 14:00 15:00 16:00 17:00
18:00 19:00 20:00 21:00 22:00 23:00 24:00** _____
_____

Spell Casting Details: _____
_____
_____
_____
_____
_____
_____
_____
_____
_____

Spell #: _____

Spell Name: _____

_____

Spell Items: _____   _____

_____   _____   _____

_____   _____   _____

_____   _____   _____

_____   _____   _____

Preferred Moon Phase: _____

Preferred Times of Day: 06:00 07:00 08:00 09:00
10:00 11:00 12:00 13:00 14:00 15:00 16:00 17:00
18:00 19:00 20:00 21:00 22:00 23:00 24:00 _____

Spell Casting Details: _____

_____

_____

_____

_____

_____

_____

_____

_____

_____

_____

Spell #: _____

Spell Name: _____

_____

Spell Items: _____ _____

_____ _____

_____ _____

_____ _____

_____ _____

Preferred Moon Phase: _____

Preferred Times of Day: 06:00 07:00 08:00 09:00
10:00 11:00 12:00 13:00 14:00 15:00 16:00 17:00
18:00 19:00 20:00 21:00 22:00 23:00 24:00 _____

_____

Spell Casting Details: _____

_____

_____

_____

_____

_____

_____

_____

_____

_____

Spell #: _____

Spell Name: _____

_____

Spell Items: _____ _____

_____ _____ _____

_____ _____ _____

_____ _____ _____

_____ _____ _____

Preferred Moon Phase:_____

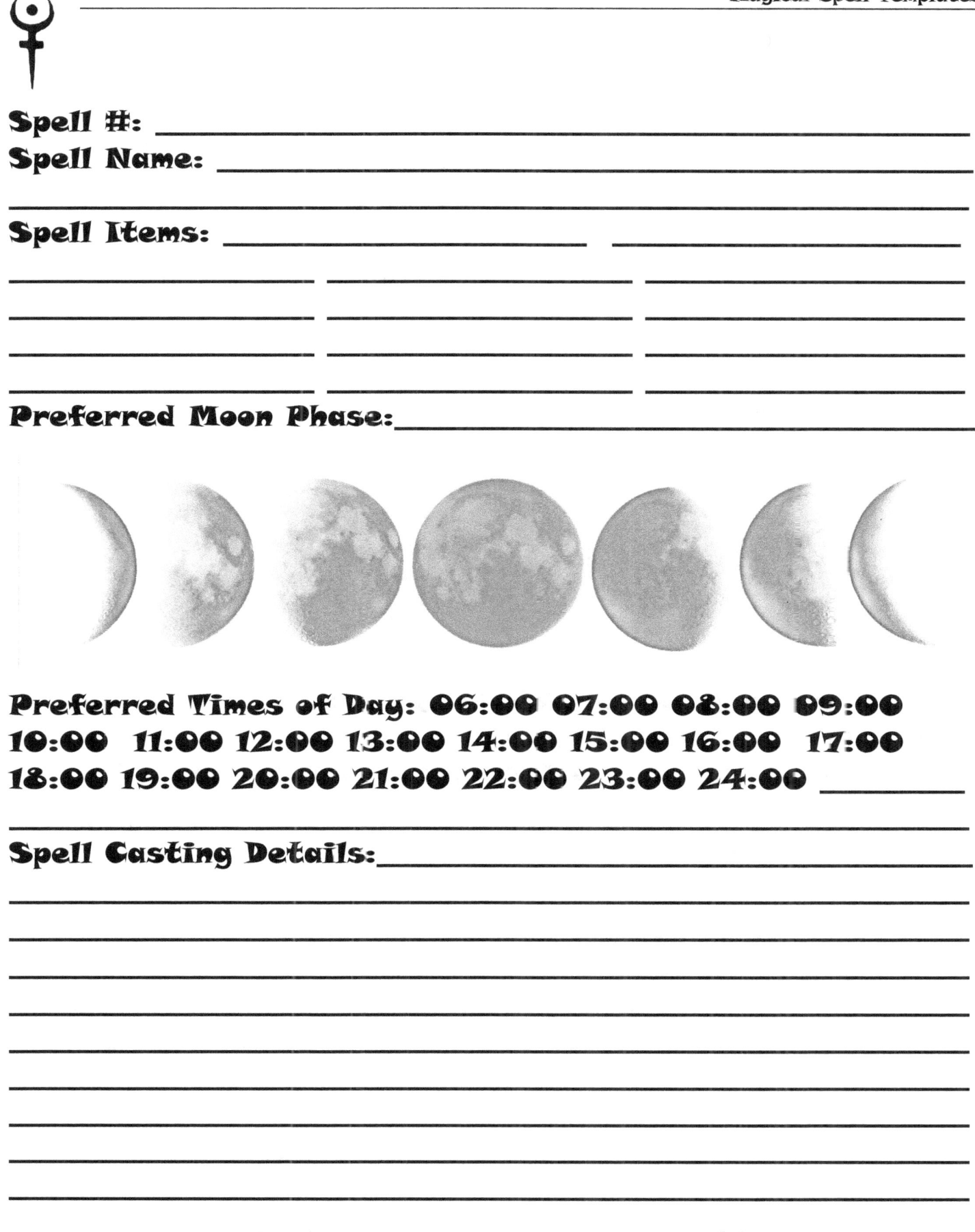

**Preferred Times of Day: 06:00 07:00 08:00 09:00
10:00 11:00 12:00 13:00 14:00 15:00 16:00 17:00
18:00 19:00 20:00 21:00 22:00 23:00 24:00** _____

_____

Spell Casting Details:_____

_____

_____

_____

_____

_____

_____

_____

_____

_____

_____

_____

Spell #: _____

Spell Name: _____

_____

Spell Items: _____ _____

_____ _____ _____

_____ _____ _____

_____ _____ _____

_____ _____ _____

Preferred Moon Phase:_____

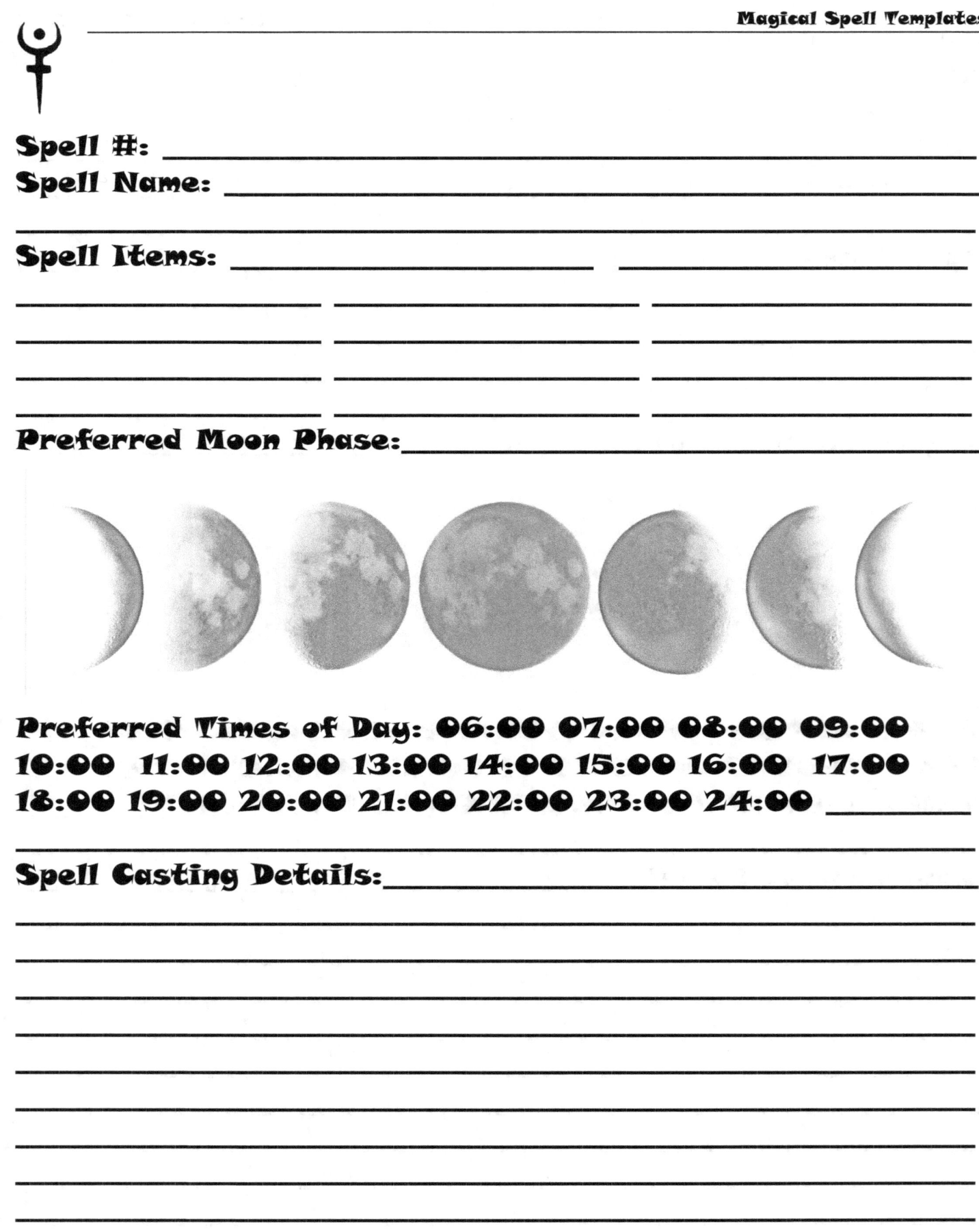

Preferred Times of Day: 06:00 07:00 08:00 09:00
10:00 11:00 12:00 13:00 14:00 15:00 16:00 17:00
18:00 19:00 20:00 21:00 22:00 23:00 24:00 _____

_____

Spell Casting Details:_____

_____

_____

_____

_____

_____

_____

_____

_____

_____

Spell #: _____

Spell Name: _____

_____

Spell Items: _____ _____

_____ _____ _____

_____ _____ _____

_____ _____ _____

_____ _____ _____

Preferred Moon Phase: _____

Preferred Times of Day: 06:00 07:00 08:00 09:00
10:00 11:00 12:00 13:00 14:00 15:00 16:00 17:00
18:00 19:00 20:00 21:00 22:00 23:00 24:00 _____

_____

Spell Casting Details: _____

_____

_____

_____

_____

_____

_____

_____

_____

_____

_____

Spell #: _____

Spell Name: _____
_____

Spell Items: _____   _____
_____   _____   _____
_____   _____   _____
_____   _____   _____
_____   _____   _____

Preferred Moon Phase: _____

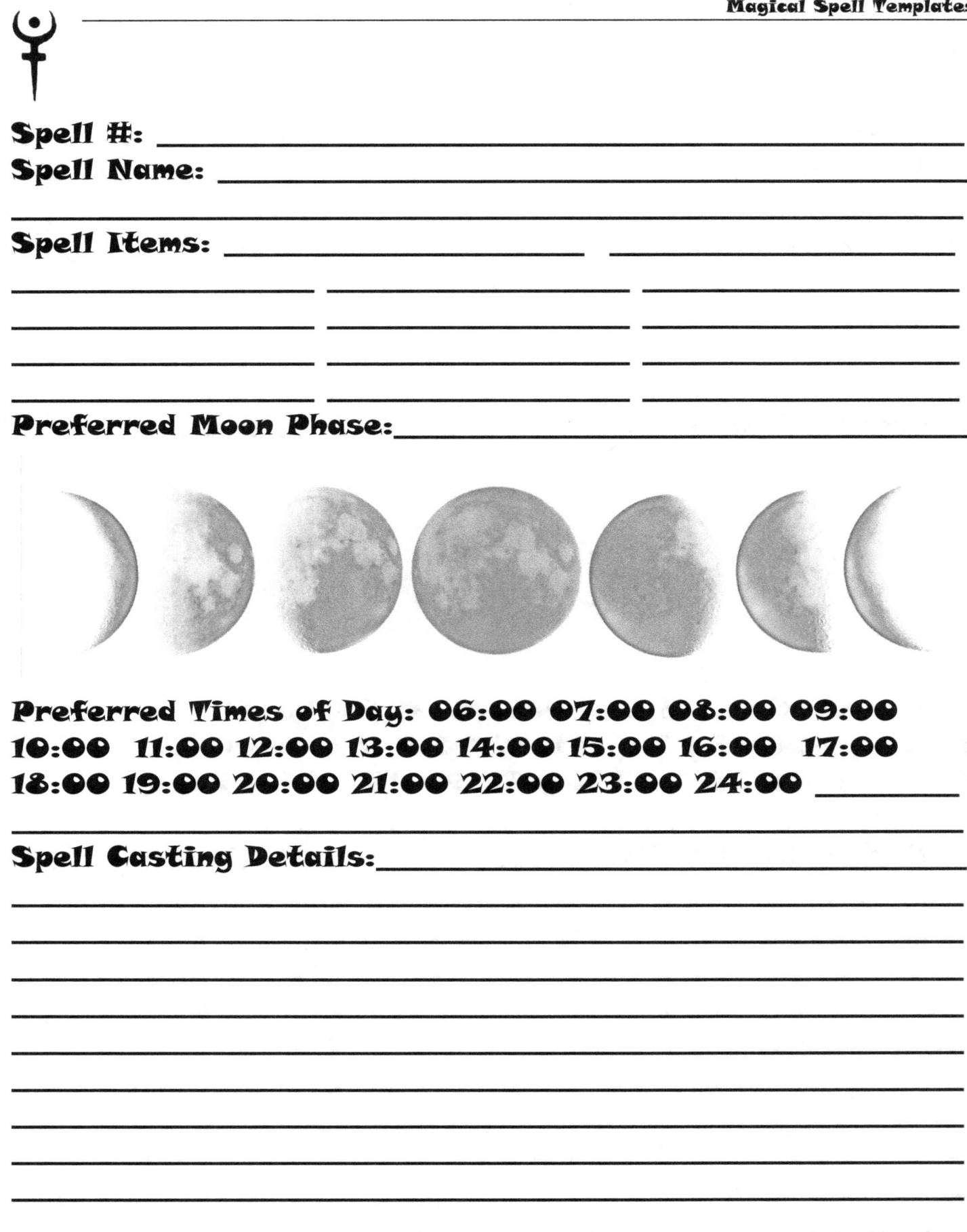

**Preferred Times of Day: 06:00 07:00 08:00 09:00
10:00 11:00 12:00 13:00 14:00 15:00 16:00 17:00
18:00 19:00 20:00 21:00 22:00 23:00 24:00** _____
_____

Spell Casting Details: _____
_____
_____
_____
_____
_____
_____
_____
_____
_____
_____

Spell #: _____

Spell Name: _____

_____

Spell Items: _____ _____

_____ _____ _____

_____ _____ _____

_____ _____ _____

_____ _____ _____

Preferred Moon Phase: _____

Preferred Times of Day: 06:00 07:00 08:00 09:00
10:00 11:00 12:00 13:00 14:00 15:00 16:00 17:00
18:00 19:00 20:00 21:00 22:00 23:00 24:00 _____

Spell Casting Details: _____

_____

_____

_____

_____

_____

_____

_____

_____

_____

_____

Spell #: _____

Spell Name: _____

_____

Spell Items: _____ _____

_____ _____

_____ _____

_____ _____

_____ _____

Preferred Moon Phase: _____

**Preferred Times of Day: 06:00 07:00 08:00 09:00
10:00 11:00 12:00 13:00 14:00 15:00 16:00 17:00
18:00 19:00 20:00 21:00 22:00 23:00 24:00** _____

_____

Spell Casting Details: _____

_____

_____

_____

_____

_____

_____

_____

_____

_____

_____

Spell #: _____

Spell Name: _____

Spell Items: _____ _____

_____ _____ _____

_____ _____ _____

_____ _____ _____

_____ _____ _____

Preferred Moon Phase: _____

Preferred Times of Day: 06:00 07:00 08:00 09:00 10:00 11:00 12:00 13:00 14:00 15:00 16:00 17:00 18:00 19:00 20:00 21:00 22:00 23:00 24:00 _____

Spell Casting Details: _____

_____

_____

_____

_____

_____

_____

_____

_____

_____

_____

Spell #: _____

Spell Name: _____
_____

Spell Items: _____ _____
_____ _____ _____
_____ _____ _____
_____ _____ _____
_____ _____ _____

Preferred Moon Phase:_____

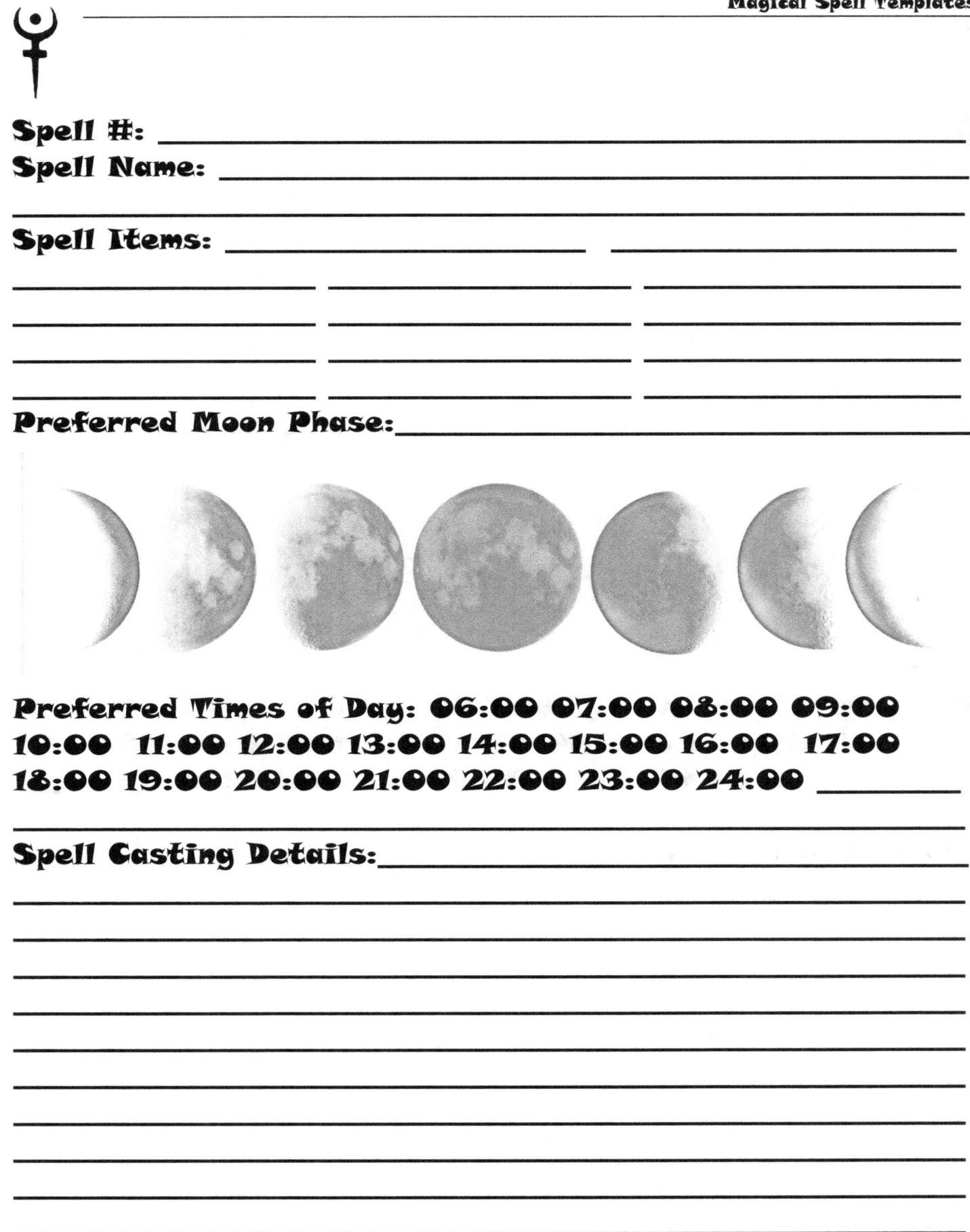

Preferred Times of Day: 06:00 07:00 08:00 09:00
10:00 11:00 12:00 13:00 14:00 15:00 16:00 17:00
18:00 19:00 20:00 21:00 22:00 23:00 24:00 _____
_____

Spell Casting Details:_____
_____
_____
_____
_____
_____
_____
_____
_____
_____
_____

Spell #: _____

Spell Name: _____

_____

Spell Items: _____   _____

_____   _____   _____

_____   _____   _____

_____   _____   _____

_____   _____   _____

Preferred Moon Phase:_____

**Preferred Times of Day: 06:00 07:00 08:00 09:00
10:00 11:00 12:00 13:00 14:00 15:00 16:00 17:00
18:00 19:00 20:00 21:00 22:00 23:00 24:00** _____

Spell Casting Details:_____

_____

_____

_____

_____

_____

_____

_____

_____

_____

Spell #: _____

Spell Name: _____
_____

Spell Items: _____ _____
_____ _____
_____ _____
_____ _____
_____ _____

Preferred Moon Phase: _____

Preferred Times of Day: 06:00 07:00 08:00 09:00
10:00 11:00 12:00 13:00 14:00 15:00 16:00 17:00
18:00 19:00 20:00 21:00 22:00 23:00 24:00 _____
_____

Spell Casting Details: _____
_____
_____
_____
_____
_____
_____
_____
_____
_____
_____

Spell #: _____

Spell Name: _____
_____

Spell Items: _____ _____
_____ _____ _____
_____ _____ _____
_____ _____ _____
_____ _____ _____

Preferred Moon Phase:_____

**Preferred Times of Day: 06:00 07:00 08:00 09:00
10:00 11:00 12:00 13:00 14:00 15:00 16:00 17:00
18:00 19:00 20:00 21:00 22:00 23:00 24:00** _____

Spell Casting Details:_____
_____
_____
_____
_____
_____
_____
_____
_____
_____
_____

Spell #: _____

Spell Name: _____
_____

Spell Items: _____ _____
_____ _____ _____
_____ _____ _____
_____ _____ _____
_____ _____ _____

Preferred Moon Phase:_____

**Preferred Times of Day: 06:00 07:00 08:00 09:00
10:00 11:00 12:00 13:00 14:00 15:00 16:00 17:00
18:00 19:00 20:00 21:00 22:00 23:00 24:00 _____**
_____

Spell Casting Details:_____
_____
_____
_____
_____
_____
_____
_____
_____
_____
_____

Spell #: _____

Spell Name: _____
_____

Spell Items: _____ _____
_____ _____ _____
_____ _____ _____
_____ _____ _____
_____ _____ _____

Preferred Moon Phase:_____

Preferred Times of Day: 06:00 07:00 08:00 09:00
10:00 11:00 12:00 13:00 14:00 15:00 16:00 17:00
18:00 19:00 20:00 21:00 22:00 23:00 24:00 _____
_____

Spell Casting Details:_____
_____
_____
_____
_____
_____
_____
_____
_____
_____
_____

Spell #: _____

Spell Name: _____
_____

Spell Items: _____ _____
_____ _____
_____ _____
_____ _____
_____ _____

Preferred Moon Phase: _____

Preferred Times of Day: 06:00 07:00 08:00 09:00
10:00 11:00 12:00 13:00 14:00 15:00 16:00 17:00
18:00 19:00 20:00 21:00 22:00 23:00 24:00 _____
_____

Spell Casting Details: _____
_____
_____
_____
_____
_____
_____
_____
_____
_____

Spell #: _____

Spell Name: _____
_____

Spell Items: _____ _____
_____ _____ _____
_____ _____ _____
_____ _____ _____
_____ _____ _____

Preferred Moon Phase: _____

Preferred Times of Day: 06:00 07:00 08:00 09:00
10:00 11:00 12:00 13:00 14:00 15:00 16:00 17:00
18:00 19:00 20:00 21:00 22:00 23:00 24:00 _____
_____

Spell Casting Details: _____
_____
_____
_____
_____
_____
_____
_____
_____
_____
_____

Spell #: _____

Spell Name: _____

_____

Spell Items: _____   _____

_____   _____   _____

_____   _____   _____

_____   _____   _____

_____   _____   _____

Preferred Moon Phase:_____

**Preferred Times of Day: 06:00 07:00 08:00 09:00
10:00 11:00 12:00 13:00 14:00 15:00 16:00 17:00
18:00 19:00 20:00 21:00 22:00 23:00 24:00 _____**

Spell Casting Details:_____

_____

_____

_____

_____

_____

_____

_____

_____

_____

Spell #: _____

Spell Name: _____
_____

Spell Items: _____ _____
_____ _____ _____
_____ _____ _____
_____ _____ _____
_____ _____ _____

Preferred Moon Phase:_____

**Preferred Times of Day: 06:00 07:00 08:00 09:00
10:00 11:00 12:00 13:00 14:00 15:00 16:00 17:00
18:00 19:00 20:00 21:00 22:00 23:00 24:00** _____

Spell Casting Details:_____
_____
_____
_____
_____
_____
_____
_____
_____
_____
_____

Spell #: _____

Spell Name: _____
_____

Spell Items: _____ _____
_____ _____ _____
_____ _____ _____
_____ _____ _____
_____ _____ _____

Preferred Moon Phase: _____

Preferred Times of Day: 06:00 07:00 08:00 09:00
10:00 11:00 12:00 13:00 14:00 15:00 16:00 17:00
18:00 19:00 20:00 21:00 22:00 23:00 24:00 _____
_____

Spell Casting Details: _____
_____
_____
_____
_____
_____
_____
_____
_____
_____

Spell #: _____

Spell Name: _____
_____

Spell Items: _____ _____
_____ _____ _____
_____ _____ _____
_____ _____ _____
_____ _____ _____

Preferred Moon Phase:_____

**Preferred Times of Day: 06:00 07:00 08:00 09:00
10:00 11:00 12:00 13:00 14:00 15:00 16:00 17:00
18:00 19:00 20:00 21:00 22:00 23:00 24:00 _____**
_____

Spell Casting Details:_____
_____
_____
_____
_____
_____
_____
_____
_____
_____
_____
_____

Spell #: _____

Spell Name: _____

_____

Spell Items: _____ _____

_____ _____ _____

_____ _____ _____

_____ _____ _____

_____ _____ _____

Preferred Moon Phase:_____

Preferred Times of Day: 06:00 07:00 08:00 09:00
10:00 11:00 12:00 13:00 14:00 15:00 16:00 17:00
18:00 19:00 20:00 21:00 22:00 23:00 24:00 _____

_____

Spell Casting Details:_____

_____

_____

_____

_____

_____

_____

_____

_____

_____

_____

Spell #: _____
Spell Name: _____
_____
Spell Items: _____ _____
_____ _____ _____
_____ _____ _____
_____ _____ _____
_____ _____ _____

Preferred Moon Phase: _____

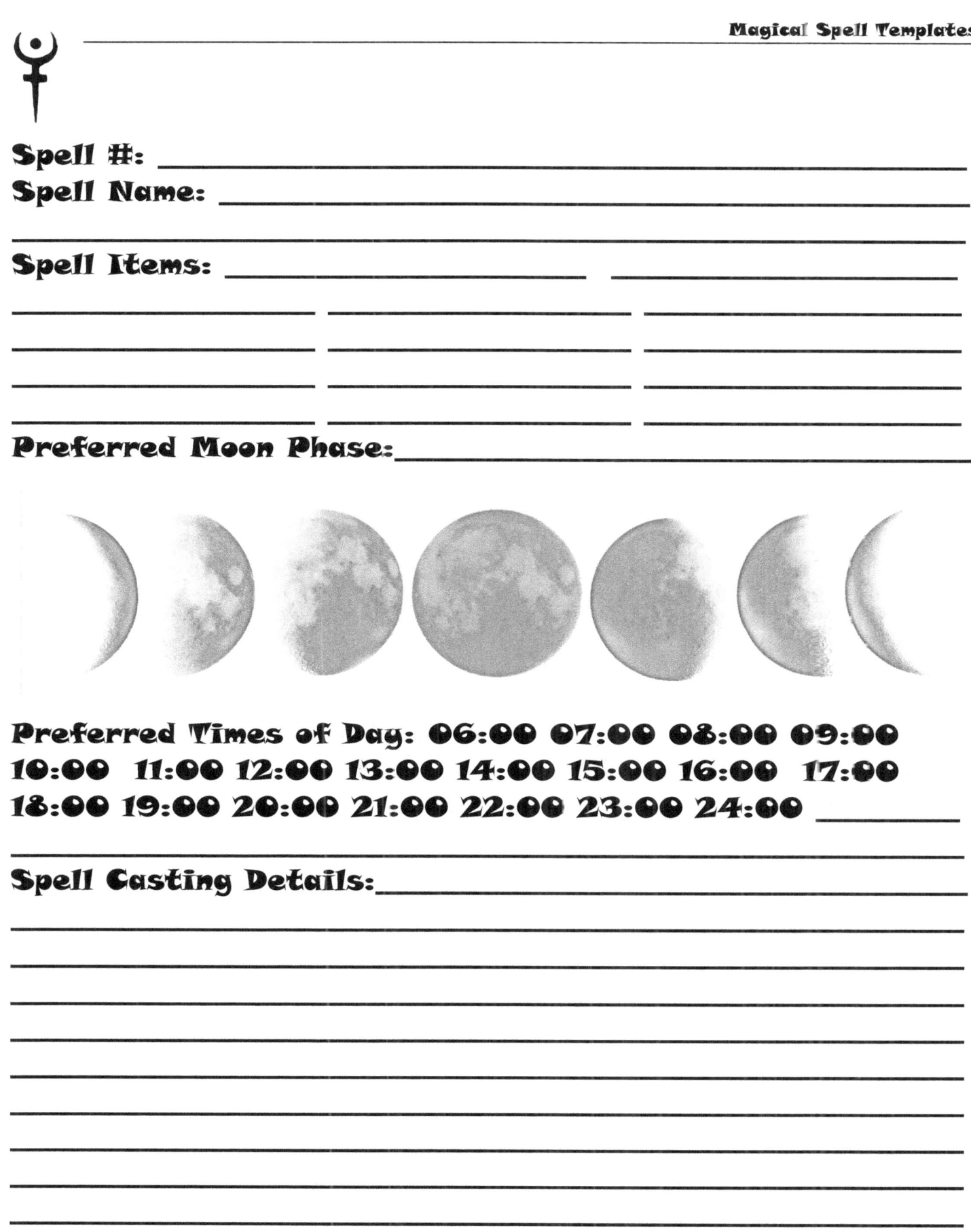

Preferred Times of Day: 06:00 07:00 08:00 09:00
10:00 11:00 12:00 13:00 14:00 15:00 16:00 17:00
18:00 19:00 20:00 21:00 22:00 23:00 24:00 _____

Spell Casting Details: _____
_____
_____
_____
_____
_____
_____
_____
_____
_____
_____
_____

Spell #: _____

Spell Name: _____
_____

Spell Items: _____ _____
_____ _____ _____
_____ _____ _____
_____ _____ _____
_____ _____ _____

Preferred Moon Phase:_____

Preferred Times of Day: 06:00 07:00 08:00 09:00
10:00 11:00 12:00 13:00 14:00 15:00 16:00 17:00
18:00 19:00 20:00 21:00 22:00 23:00 24:00 _____
_____

Spell Casting Details:_____
_____
_____
_____
_____
_____
_____
_____
_____
_____
_____

Spell #: _____

Spell Name: _____

_____

Spell Items: _____ _____

_____ _____ _____

_____ _____ _____

_____ _____ _____

Preferred Moon Phase: _____

Preferred Times of Day: 06:00 07:00 08:00 09:00 10:00 11:00 12:00 13:00 14:00 15:00 16:00 17:00 18:00 19:00 20:00 21:00 22:00 23:00 24:00 _____

Spell Casting Details: _____

_____

_____

_____

_____

_____

_____

_____

_____

_____

_____

Spell #: _____

Spell Name: _____

_____

Spell Items: _____ _____

_____ _____ _____

_____ _____ _____

_____ _____ _____

_____ _____ _____

Preferred Moon Phase: _____

Preferred Times of Day: 06:00 07:00 08:00 09:00
10:00 11:00 12:00 13:00 14:00 15:00 16:00 17:00
18:00 19:00 20:00 21:00 22:00 23:00 24:00 _____

_____

Spell Casting Details: _____

_____

_____

_____

_____

_____

_____

_____

_____

_____

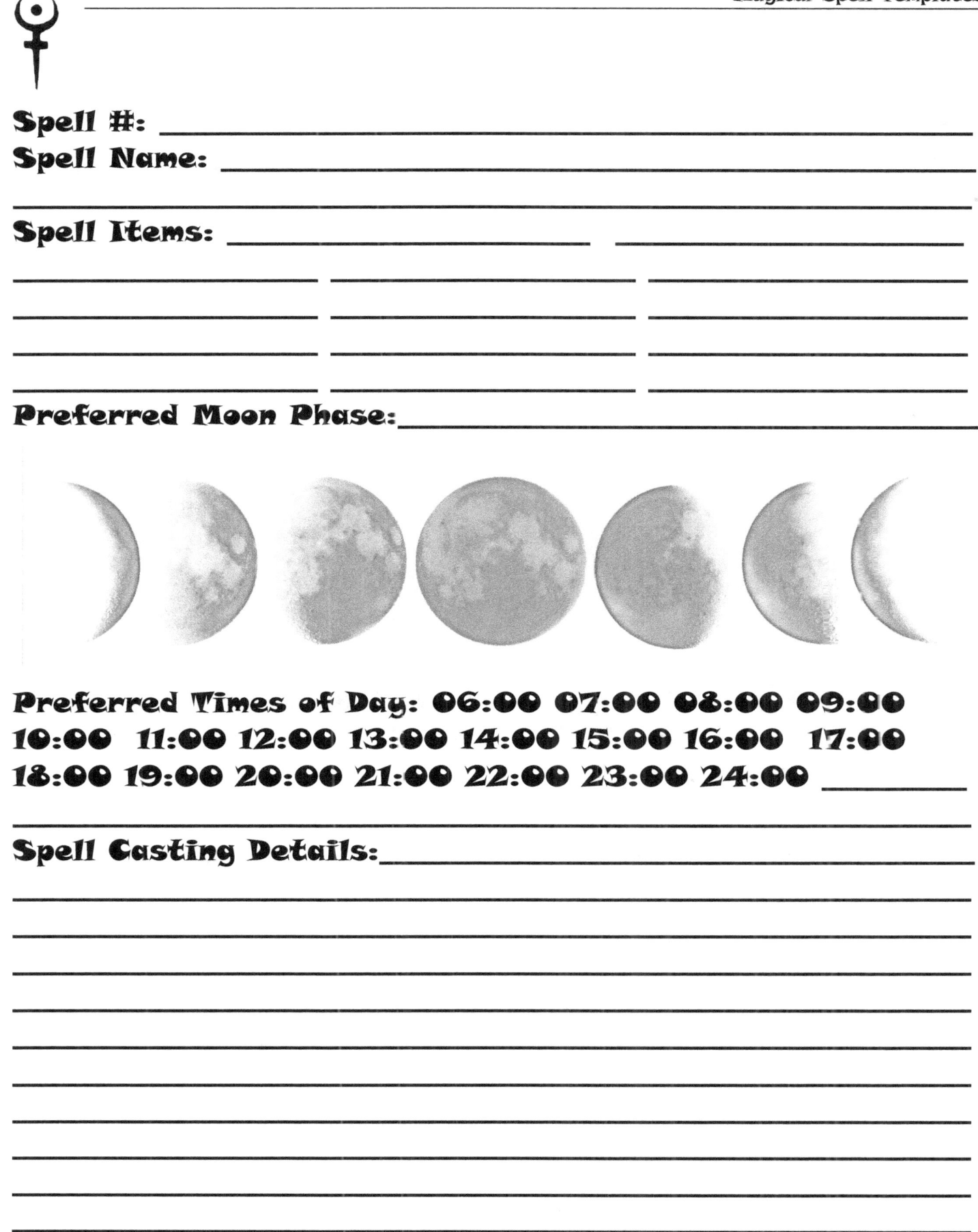

Spell #: _____

Spell Name: _____
_____

Spell Items: _____ _____
_____ _____
_____ _____
_____ _____
_____ _____

Preferred Moon Phase: _____

Preferred Times of Day: 06:00 07:00 08:00 09:00
10:00 11:00 12:00 13:00 14:00 15:00 16:00 17:00
18:00 19:00 20:00 21:00 22:00 23:00 24:00 _____

Spell Casting Details: _____
_____
_____
_____
_____
_____
_____
_____
_____
_____
_____
_____

Spell #: _____

Spell Name: _____

_____

Spell Items: _____   _____

_____   _____   _____

_____   _____   _____

_____   _____   _____

_____   _____   _____

Preferred Moon Phase:_____

Preferred Times of Day: 06:00 07:00 08:00 09:00
10:00 11:00 12:00 13:00 14:00 15:00 16:00 17:00
18:00 19:00 20:00 21:00 22:00 23:00 24:00 _____

_____

Spell Casting Details:_____

_____

_____

_____

_____

_____

_____

_____

_____

_____

_____

Spell #: _____

Spell Name: _____

_____

Spell Items: _____   _____

_____   _____   _____

_____   _____   _____

_____   _____   _____

_____   _____   _____

Preferred Moon Phase: _____

Preferred Times of Day: 06:00 07:00 08:00 09:00
10:00 11:00 12:00 13:00 14:00 15:00 16:00 17:00
18:00 19:00 20:00 21:00 22:00 23:00 24:00 _____

_____

Spell Casting Details: _____

_____

_____

_____

_____

_____

_____

_____

_____

_____

_____

Spell #: _____

Spell Name: _____
_____

Spell Items: _____ _____
_____ _____ _____
_____ _____ _____
_____ _____ _____
_____ _____ _____

Preferred Moon Phase:_____

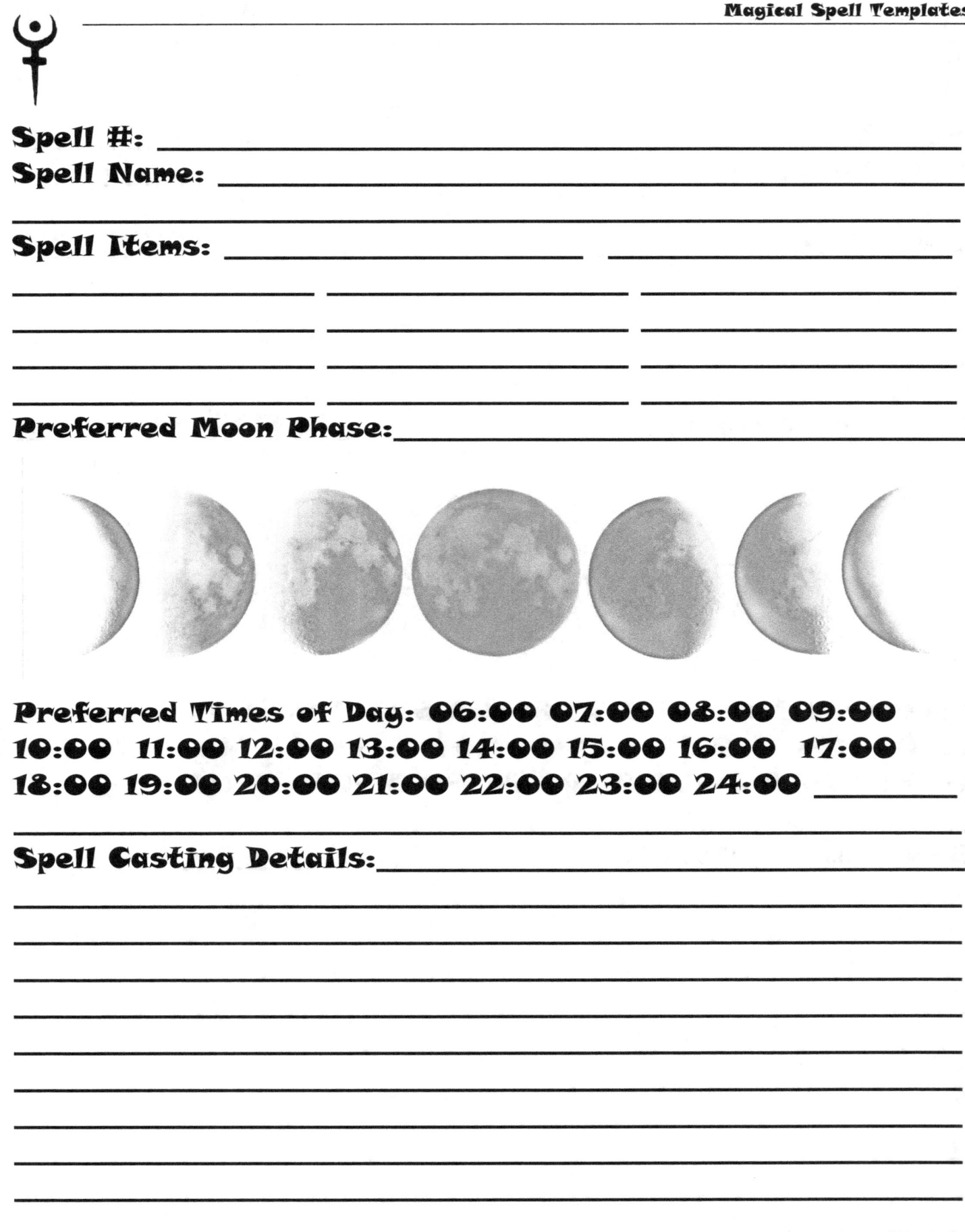

**Preferred Times of Day: 06:00 07:00 08:00 09:00
10:00 11:00 12:00 13:00 14:00 15:00 16:00 17:00
18:00 19:00 20:00 21:00 22:00 23:00 24:00** _____
_____

Spell Casting Details:_____
_____
_____
_____
_____
_____
_____
_____
_____
_____

Spell #: _____

Spell Name: _____
_____

Spell Items: _____ _____
_____ _____
_____ _____
_____ _____

Preferred Moon Phase: _____

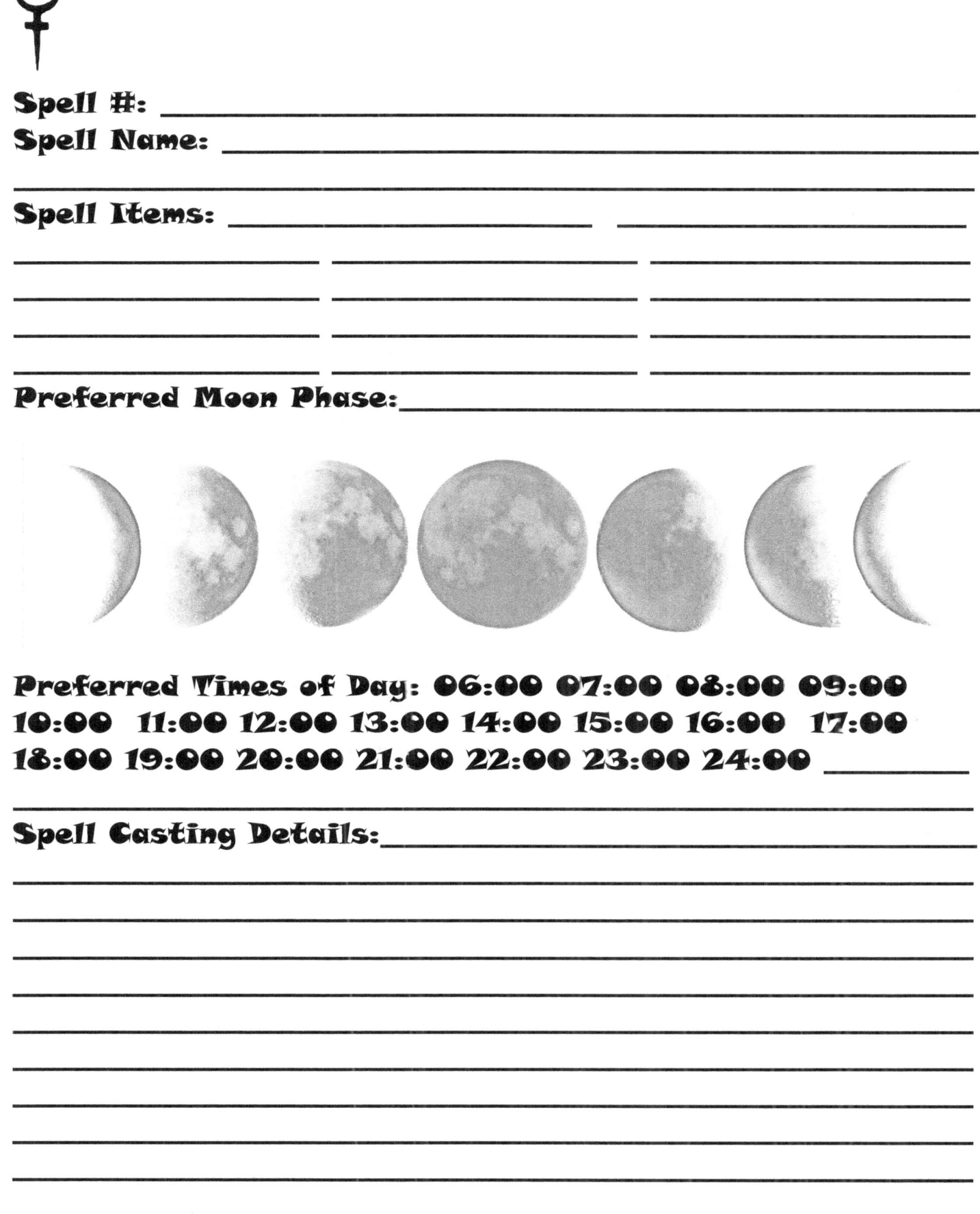

Preferred Times of Day: 06:00 07:00 08:00 09:00
10:00 11:00 12:00 13:00 14:00 15:00 16:00 17:00
18:00 19:00 20:00 21:00 22:00 23:00 24:00 _____
_____

Spell Casting Details: _____
_____
_____
_____
_____
_____
_____
_____
_____
_____
_____
_____

Spell #: _____

Spell Name: _____
_____

Spell Items: _____ _____
_____ _____
_____ _____
_____ _____
_____ _____

Preferred Moon Phase: _____

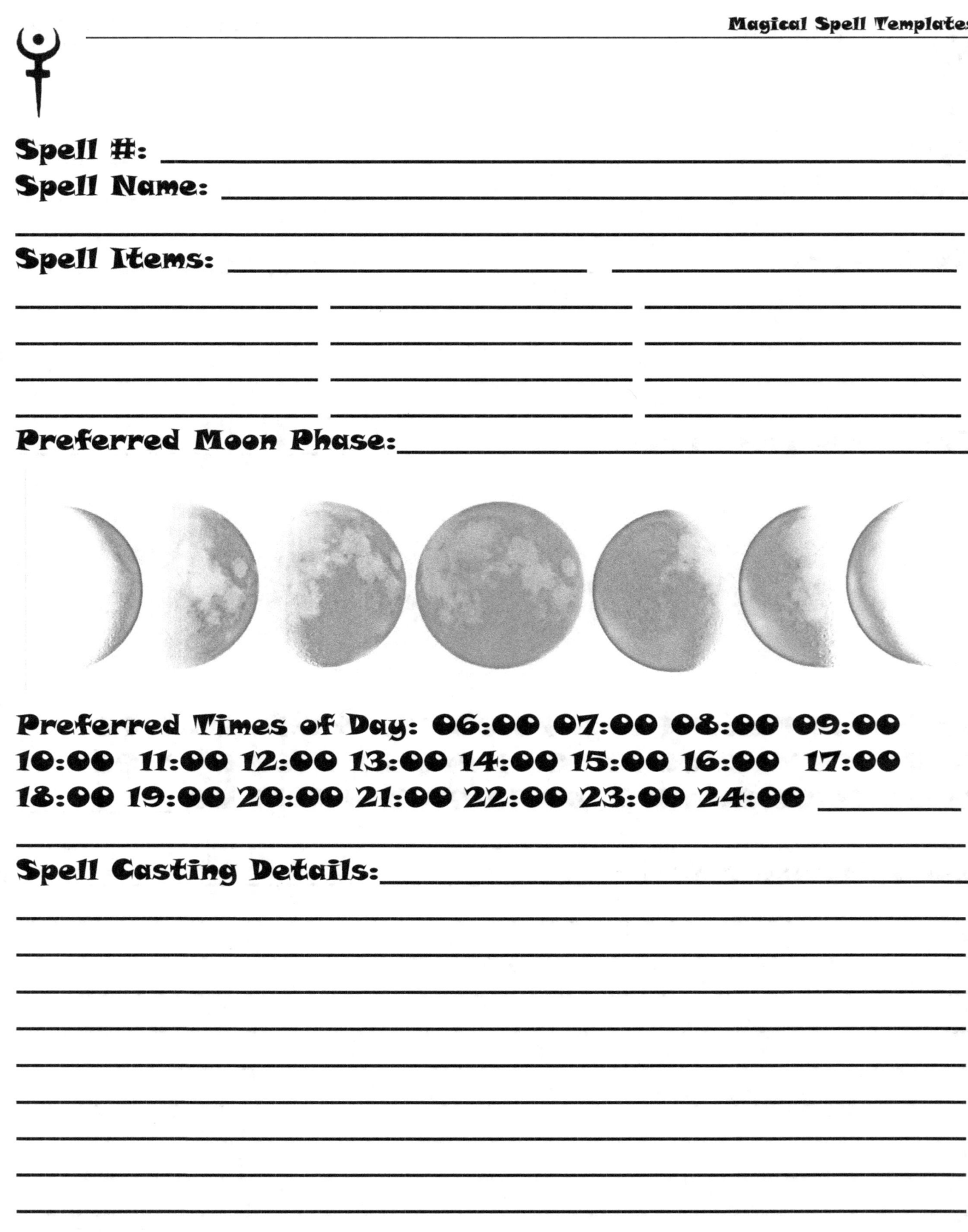

**Preferred Times of Day: 06:00 07:00 08:00 09:00
10:00 11:00 12:00 13:00 14:00 15:00 16:00 17:00
18:00 19:00 20:00 21:00 22:00 23:00 24:00 _____**

Spell Casting Details: _____
_____
_____
_____
_____
_____
_____
_____
_____
_____
_____

Spell #: _____

Spell Name: _____

_____

Spell Items: _____ _____

_____ _____ _____

_____ _____ _____

_____ _____ _____

Preferred Moon Phase:_____

Preferred Times of Day: 06:00 07:00 08:00 09:00
10:00 11:00 12:00 13:00 14:00 15:00 16:00 17:00
18:00 19:00 20:00 21:00 22:00 23:00 24:00 _____

_____

Spell Casting Details:_____

_____

_____

_____

_____

_____

_____

_____

_____

_____

Spell #: _____

Spell Name: _____

_____

Spell Items: _____ _____

_____ _____ _____

_____ _____ _____

_____ _____ _____

_____ _____ _____

Preferred Moon Phase:_____

Preferred Times of Day: 06:00 07:00 08:00 09:00 10:00 11:00 12:00 13:00 14:00 15:00 16:00 17:00 18:00 19:00 20:00 21:00 22:00 23:00 24:00 _____

_____

Spell Casting Details:_____

_____

_____

_____

_____

_____

_____

_____

_____

_____

Spell #: _____

Spell Name: _____
_____

Spell Items: _____ _____
_____ _____ _____
_____ _____ _____
_____ _____ _____
_____ _____ _____

Preferred Moon Phase:_____

Preferred Times of Day: 06:00 07:00 08:00 09:00
10:00 11:00 12:00 13:00 14:00 15:00 16:00 17:00
18:00 19:00 20:00 21:00 22:00 23:00 24:00 _____
_____

Spell Casting Details:_____
_____
_____
_____
_____
_____
_____
_____
_____
_____
_____

Spell #: _____

Spell Name: _____
_____

Spell Items: _____ _____
_____ _____
_____ _____
_____ _____
_____ _____

Preferred Moon Phase:_____

Preferred Times of Day: 06:00 07:00 08:00 09:00
10:00 11:00 12:00 13:00 14:00 15:00 16:00 17:00
18:00 19:00 20:00 21:00 22:00 23:00 24:00 _____
_____

Spell Casting Details:_____
_____
_____
_____
_____
_____
_____
_____
_____
_____
_____

Spell #: _____

Spell Name: _____

_____

Spell Items: _____   _____

_____   _____   _____

_____   _____   _____

_____   _____   _____

_____   _____   _____

Preferred Moon Phase:_____

**Preferred Times of Day: 06:00 07:00 08:00 09:00
10:00 11:00 12:00 13:00 14:00 15:00 16:00 17:00
18:00 19:00 20:00 21:00 22:00 23:00 24:00** _____

_____

Spell Casting Details:_____

_____

_____

_____

_____

_____

_____

_____

_____

_____

_____

Spell #: _____

Spell Name: _____

_____

Spell Items: _____ _____

_____ _____ _____

_____ _____ _____

_____ _____ _____

Preferred Moon Phase: _____

Preferred Times of Day: **06:00 07:00 08:00 09:00
10:00 11:00 12:00 13:00 14:00 15:00 16:00 17:00
18:00 19:00 20:00 21:00 22:00 23:00 24:00** _____

_____

Spell Casting Details: _____

_____

_____

_____

_____

_____

_____

_____

_____

_____

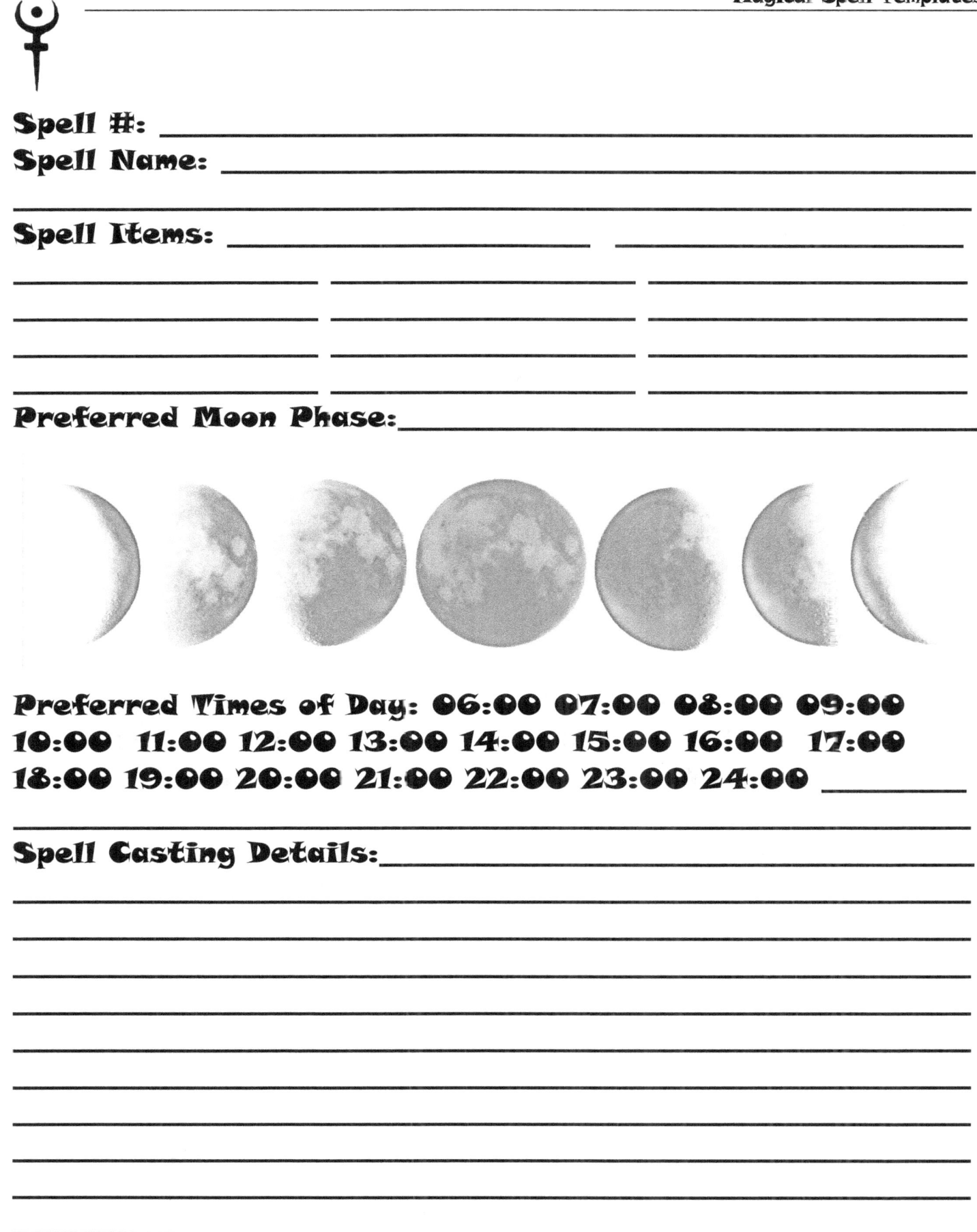

Spell #: _____

Spell Name: _____

_____

Spell Items: _____   _____

_____   _____   _____

_____   _____   _____

_____   _____   _____

_____   _____   _____

Preferred Moon Phase: _____

**Preferred Times of Day: 06:00 07:00 08:00 09:00
10:00 11:00 12:00 13:00 14:00 15:00 16:00 17:00
18:00 19:00 20:00 21:00 22:00 23:00 24:00 _____**

_____

Spell Casting Details: _____

_____

_____

_____

_____

_____

_____

_____

_____

_____

_____

Spell #: _____

Spell Name: _____

_____

Spell Items: _____ _____

_____ _____ _____

_____ _____ _____

_____ _____ _____

_____ _____ _____

Preferred Moon Phase:_____

Preferred Times of Day: **06:00 07:00 08:00 09:00**
10:00 11:00 12:00 13:00 14:00 15:00 16:00 17:00
18:00 19:00 20:00 21:00 22:00 23:00 24:00 _____

_____

Spell Casting Details:_____

_____

_____

_____

_____

_____

_____

_____

_____

_____

_____

Spell #: _____

Spell Name: _____

Spell Items: _____ _____

_____ _____

_____ _____

_____ _____

Preferred Moon Phase:_____

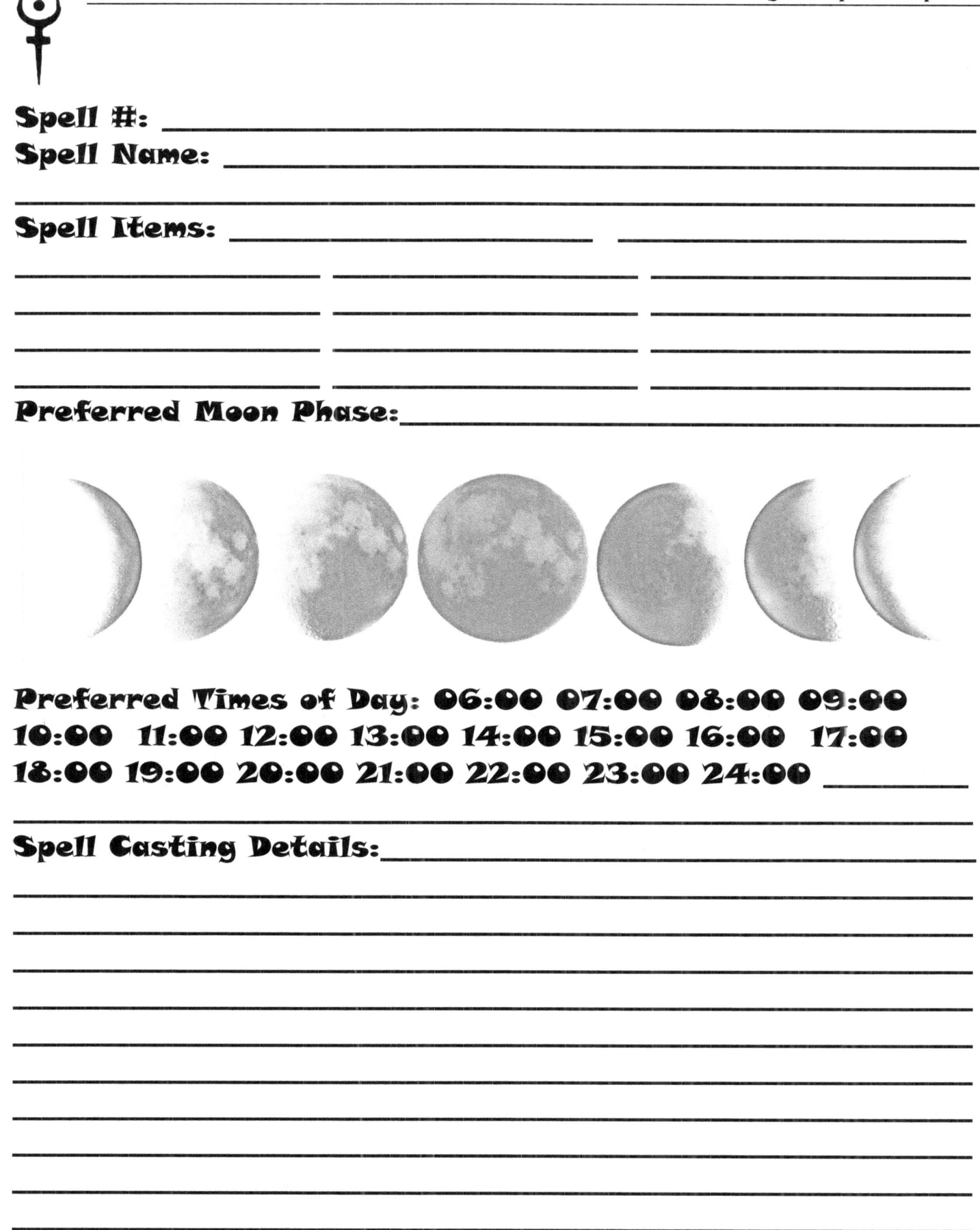

Preferred Times of Day: 06:00 07:00 08:00 09:00
10:00 11:00 12:00 13:00 14:00 15:00 16:00 17:00
18:00 19:00 20:00 21:00 22:00 23:00 24:00 _____

Spell Casting Details:_____

_____

_____

_____

_____

_____

_____

_____

_____

_____

_____

Spell #: _____

Spell Name: _____

_____

Spell Items: _____ _____

_____ _____

_____ _____

_____ _____

_____ _____

Preferred Moon Phase: _____

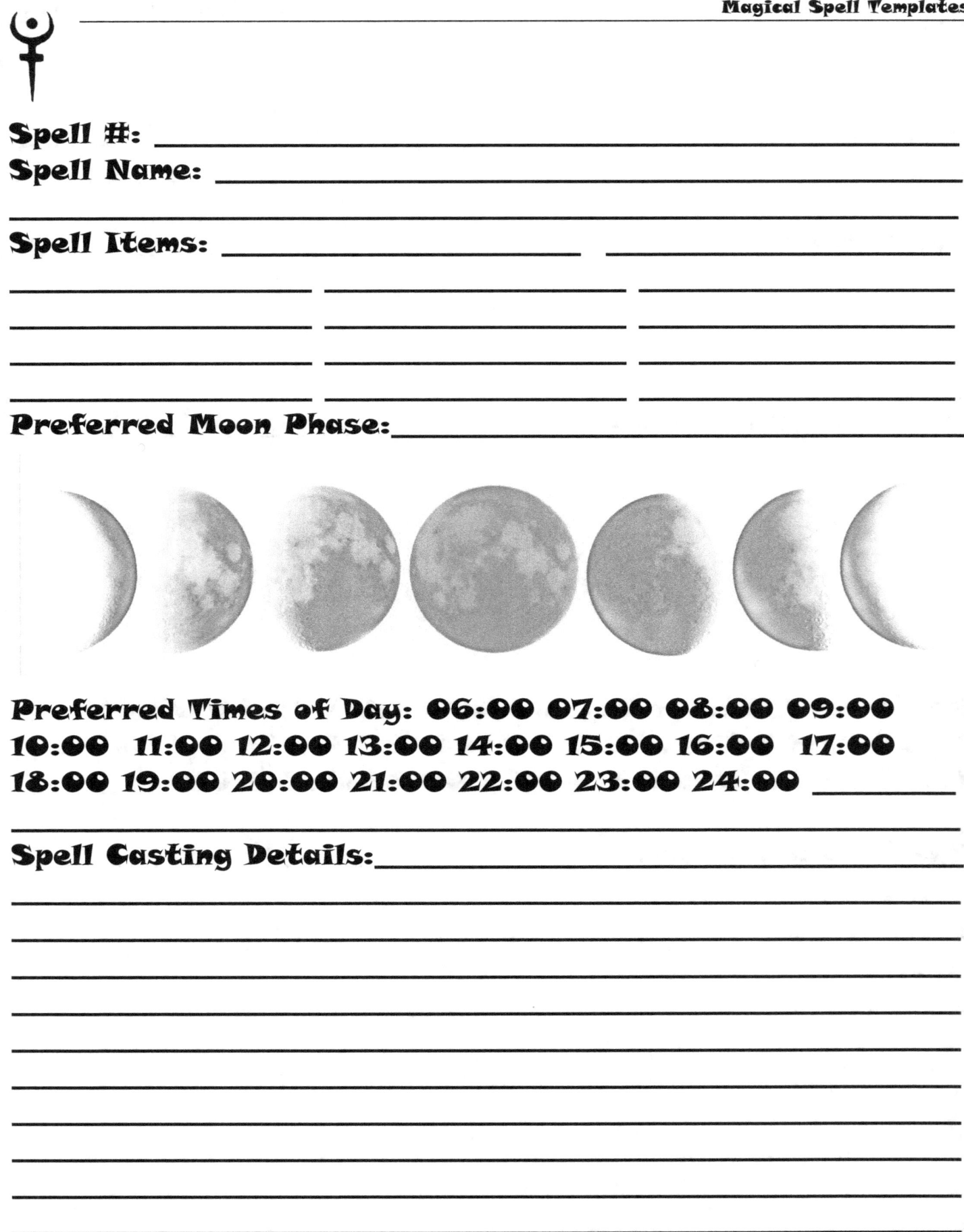

Preferred Times of Day: 06:00 07:00 08:00 09:00
10:00 11:00 12:00 13:00 14:00 15:00 16:00 17:00
18:00 19:00 20:00 21:00 22:00 23:00 24:00 _____

_____

Spell Casting Details: _____

_____

_____

_____

_____

_____

_____

_____

_____

_____

_____

Spell #: _____

Spell Name: _____
_____

Spell Items: _____   _____

_____   _____   _____

_____   _____   _____

_____   _____   _____

_____   _____   _____

Preferred Moon Phase:_____

Preferred Times of Day: 06:00 07:00 08:00 09:00
10:00 11:00 12:00 13:00 14:00 15:00 16:00 17:00
18:00 19:00 20:00 21:00 22:00 23:00 24:00 _____
_____

Spell Casting Details:_____
_____
_____
_____
_____
_____
_____
_____
_____
_____
_____
_____

Spell #: _____

Spell Name: _____

_____

Spell Items: _____ _____

_____ _____ _____

_____ _____ _____

_____ _____ _____

_____ _____ _____

Preferred Moon Phase: _____

Preferred Times of Day: **06:00 07:00 08:00 09:00**
10:00 11:00 12:00 13:00 14:00 15:00 16:00 17:00
18:00 19:00 20:00 21:00 22:00 23:00 24:00 _____

_____

Spell Casting Details: _____

_____

_____

_____

_____

_____

_____

_____

_____

_____

_____

Spell #: _____

Spell Name: _____

_____

Spell Items: _____ _____

_____ _____ _____

_____ _____ _____

_____ _____ _____

_____ _____ _____

Preferred Moon Phase:_____

Preferred Times of Day: 06:00 07:00 08:00 09:00
10:00 11:00 12:00 13:00 14:00 15:00 16:00 17:00
18:00 19:00 20:00 21:00 22:00 23:00 24:00 _____

_____

Spell Casting Details:_____

_____

_____

_____

_____

_____

_____

_____

_____

_____

_____

Spell #: _____

Spell Name: _____
_____

Spell Items: _____   _____
_____   _____   _____
_____   _____   _____
_____   _____   _____
_____   _____   _____

Preferred Moon Phase:_____

**Preferred Times of Day: 06:00 07:00 08:00 09:00
10:00 11:00 12:00 13:00 14:00 15:00 16:00 17:00
18:00 19:00 20:00 21:00 22:00 23:00 24:00 _____**
_____

Spell Casting Details:_____
_____
_____
_____
_____
_____
_____
_____
_____
_____
_____

Spell #: _____

Spell Name: _____

_____

Spell Items: _____ _____

_____ _____ _____

_____ _____ _____

_____ _____ _____

_____ _____ _____

Preferred Moon Phase: _____

Preferred Times of Day: 06:00 07:00 08:00 09:00
10:00 11:00 12:00 13:00 14:00 15:00 16:00 17:00
18:00 19:00 20:00 21:00 22:00 23:00 24:00 _____

_____

Spell Casting Details: _____

_____

_____

_____

_____

_____

_____

_____

_____

_____

_____

Spell #: _____

Spell Name: _____

_____

Spell Items: _____   _____

_____   _____   _____

_____   _____   _____

_____   _____   _____

_____   _____   _____

Preferred Moon Phase:_____

Preferred Times of Day: 06:00 07:00 08:00 09:00
10:00 11:00 12:00 13:00 14:00 15:00 16:00 17:00
18:00 19:00 20:00 21:00 22:00 23:00 24:00 _____

_____

Spell Casting Details:_____

_____

_____

_____

_____

_____

_____

_____

_____

_____

_____

Spell #: _____

Spell Name: _____

_____

Spell Items: _____ _____

_____ _____

_____ _____

_____ _____

Preferred Moon Phase: _____

Preferred Times of Day: 06:00 07:00 08:00 09:00
10:00 11:00 12:00 13:00 14:00 15:00 16:00 17:00
18:00 19:00 20:00 21:00 22:00 23:00 24:00 _____

_____

Spell Casting Details: _____

_____

_____

_____

_____

_____

_____

_____

_____

_____

_____

Spell #: _____

Spell Name: _____

_____

Spell Items: _____ _____

_____ _____ _____

_____ _____ _____

_____ _____ _____

_____ _____ _____

Preferred Moon Phase:_____

Preferred Times of Day: 06:00 07:00 08:00 09:00 10:00 11:00 12:00 13:00 14:00 15:00 16:00 17:00 18:00 19:00 20:00 21:00 22:00 23:00 24:00 _____

_____

Spell Casting Details:_____

_____

_____

_____

_____

_____

_____

_____

_____

_____

Spell #: _____

Spell Name: _____

_____

Spell Items: _____ _____

_____ _____ _____

_____ _____ _____

_____ _____ _____

_____ _____ _____

Preferred Moon Phase: _____

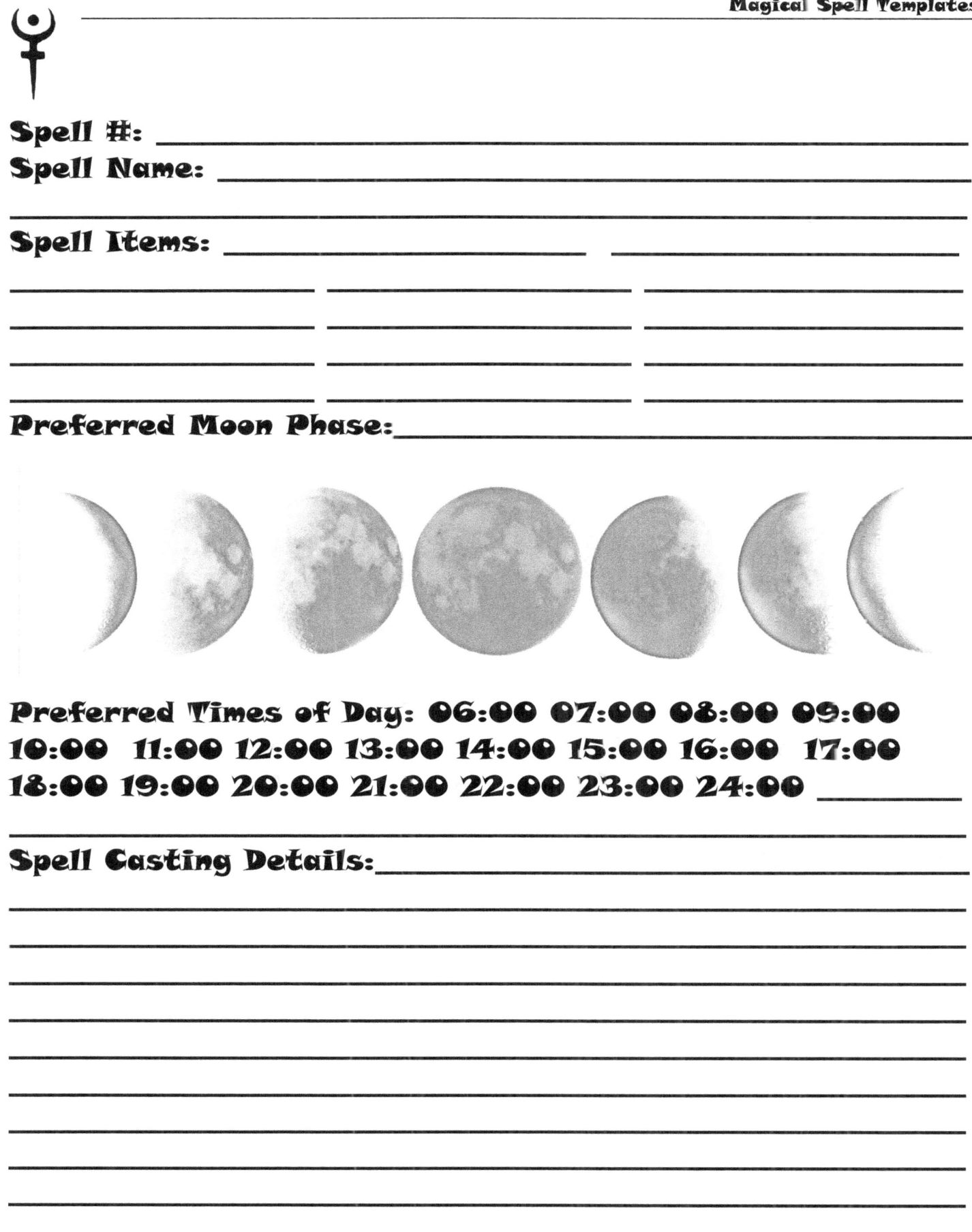

**Preferred Times of Day: 06:00 07:00 08:00 09:00
10:00 11:00 12:00 13:00 14:00 15:00 16:00 17:00
18:00 19:00 20:00 21:00 22:00 23:00 24:00** _____

_____

Spell Casting Details: _____

_____

_____

_____

_____

_____

_____

_____

_____

_____

_____

Spell #: _____

Spell Name: _____

_____

Spell Items: _____   _____

_____   _____

_____   _____

_____   _____

_____   _____

Preferred Moon Phase: _____

Preferred Times of Day: 06:00 07:00 08:00 09:00
10:00 11:00 12:00 13:00 14:00 15:00 16:00 17:00
18:00 19:00 20:00 21:00 22:00 23:00 24:00 _____

_____

Spell Casting Details: _____

_____

_____

_____

_____

_____

_____

_____

_____

_____

_____

Spell #: _____

Spell Name: _____
_____

Spell Items: _____ _____

_____ _____ _____

_____ _____ _____

_____ _____ _____

_____ _____ _____

Preferred Moon Phase: _____

Preferred Times of Day: 06:00 07:00 08:00 09:00
10:00 11:00 12:00 13:00 14:00 15:00 16:00 17:00
18:00 19:00 20:00 21:00 22:00 23:00 24:00 _____

_____

Spell Casting Details: _____

_____
_____
_____
_____
_____
_____
_____
_____
_____
_____

Spell #: _____

Spell Name: _____

_____

Spell Items: _____   _____

_____   _____

_____   _____

_____   _____

_____   _____

Preferred Moon Phase: _____

**Preferred Times of Day: 06:00 07:00 08:00 09:00
10:00 11:00 12:00 13:00 14:00 15:00 16:00 17:00
18:00 19:00 20:00 21:00 22:00 23:00 24:00** _____

_____

Spell Casting Details: _____

_____

_____

_____

_____

_____

_____

_____

_____

_____

Spell #: _____
Spell Name: _____
_____

Spell Items: _____ _____
_____ _____ _____
_____ _____ _____
_____ _____ _____
_____ _____ _____

Preferred Moon Phase: _____

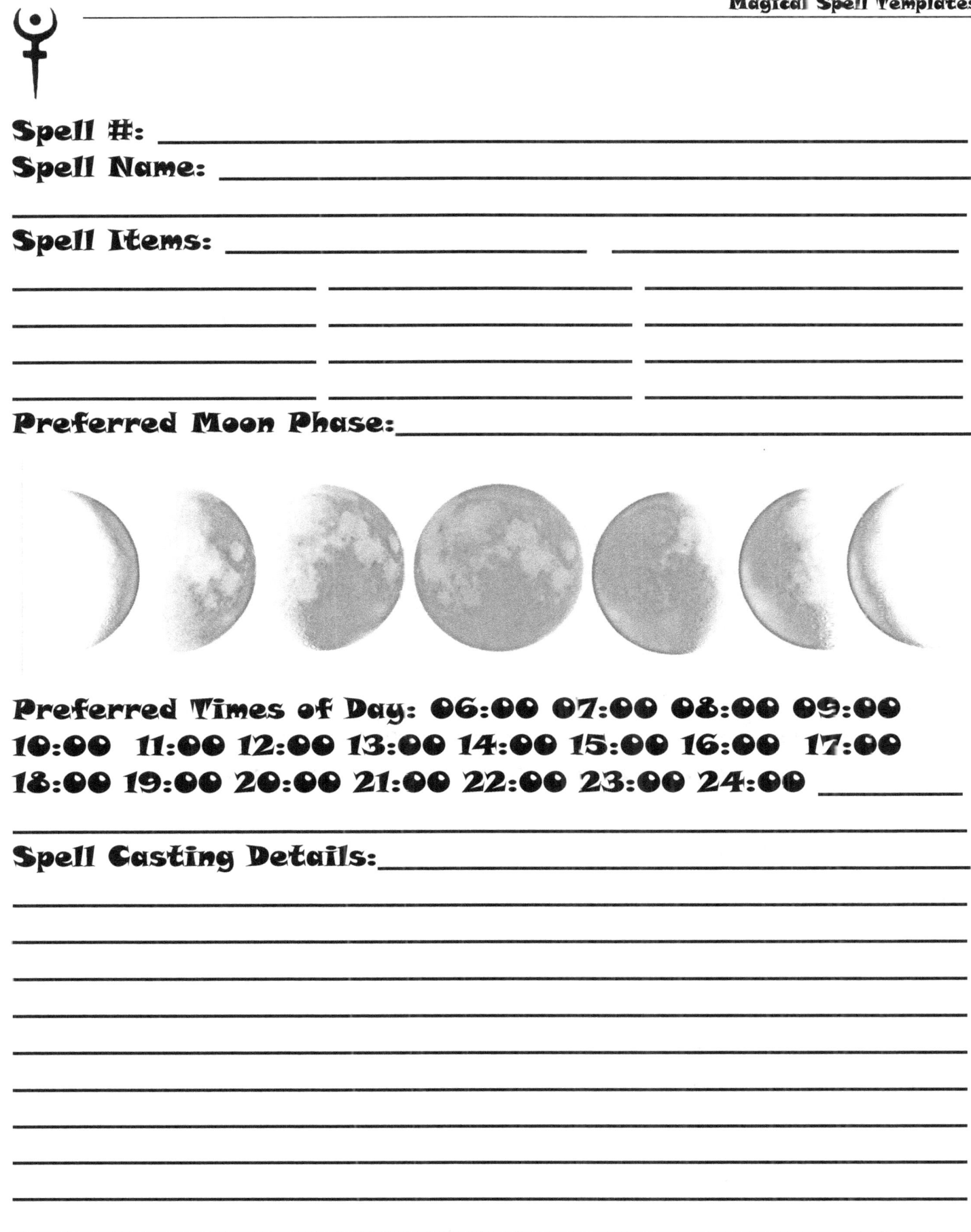

Preferred Times of Day: 06:00 07:00 08:00 09:00
10:00 11:00 12:00 13:00 14:00 15:00 16:00 17:00
18:00 19:00 20:00 21:00 22:00 23:00 24:00 _____
_____

Spell Casting Details: _____
_____
_____
_____
_____
_____
_____
_____
_____
_____
_____
_____

Spell #: _____

Spell Name: _____
_____

Spell Items: _____ _____
_____ _____ _____
_____ _____ _____
_____ _____ _____
_____ _____ _____

Preferred Moon Phase: _____

Preferred Times of Day: 06:00 07:00 08:00 09:00
10:00 11:00 12:00 13:00 14:00 15:00 16:00 17:00
18:00 19:00 20:00 21:00 22:00 23:00 24:00 _____
_____

Spell Casting Details: _____
_____
_____
_____
_____
_____
_____
_____
_____
_____
_____
_____

Spell #: _____

Spell Name: _____

_____

Spell Items: _____ _____

_____ _____ _____

_____ _____ _____

_____ _____ _____

_____ _____ _____

Preferred Moon Phase: _____

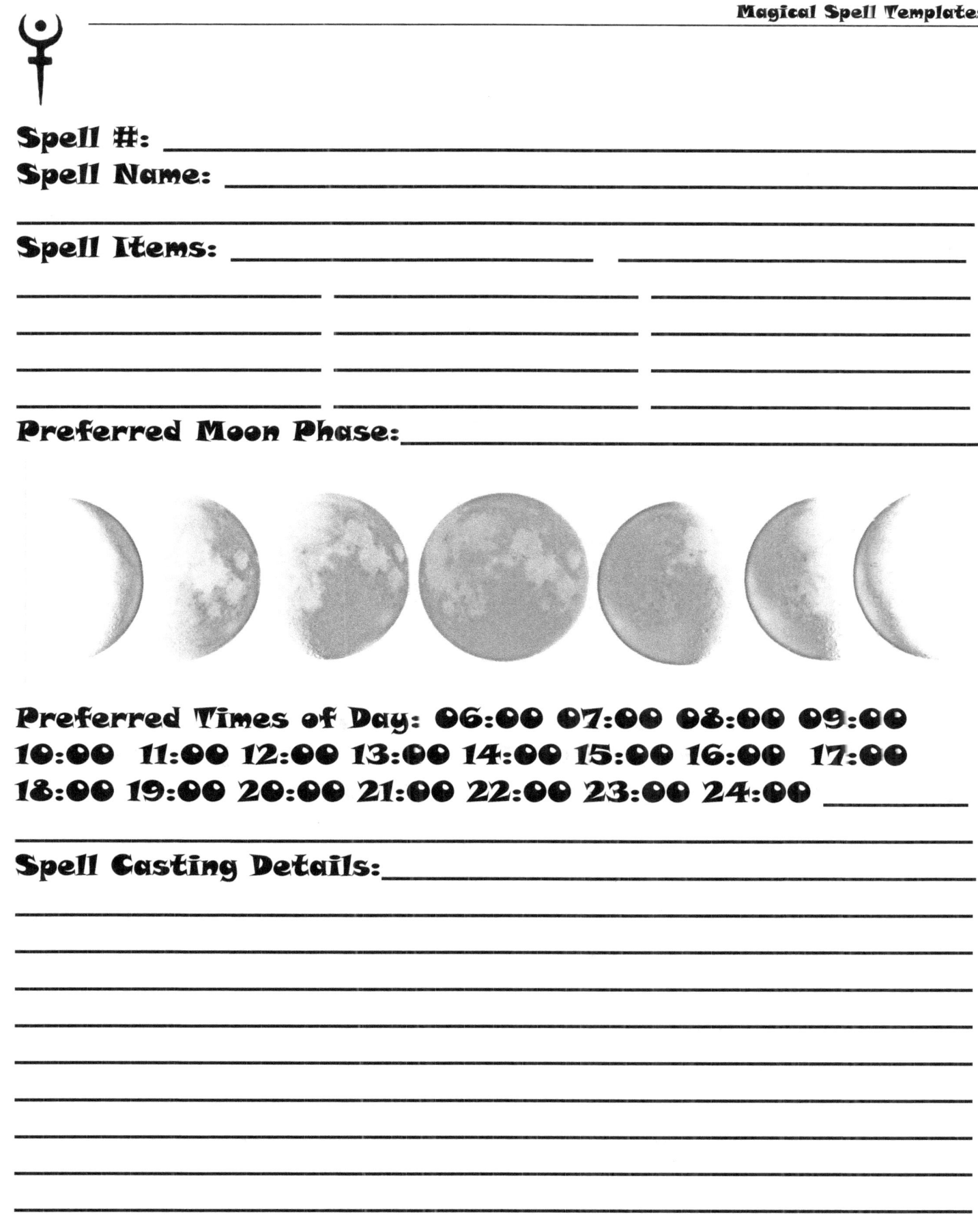

**Preferred Times of Day: 06:00 07:00 08:00 09:00
10:00 11:00 12:00 13:00 14:00 15:00 16:00 17:00
18:00 19:00 20:00 21:00 22:00 23:00 24:00 _____**

Spell Casting Details: _____

_____

_____

_____

_____

_____

_____

_____

_____

_____

_____

_____

Spell #: _____

Spell Name: _____

_____

Spell Items: _____ _____

_____ _____ _____

_____ _____ _____

_____ _____ _____

_____ _____ _____

Preferred Moon Phase:_____

**Preferred Times of Day: 06:00 07:00 08:00 09:00
10:00 11:00 12:00 13:00 14:00 15:00 16:00 17:00
18:00 19:00 20:00 21:00 22:00 23:00 24:00 _____**

_____

Spell Casting Details:_____

_____

_____

_____

_____

_____

_____

_____

_____

_____

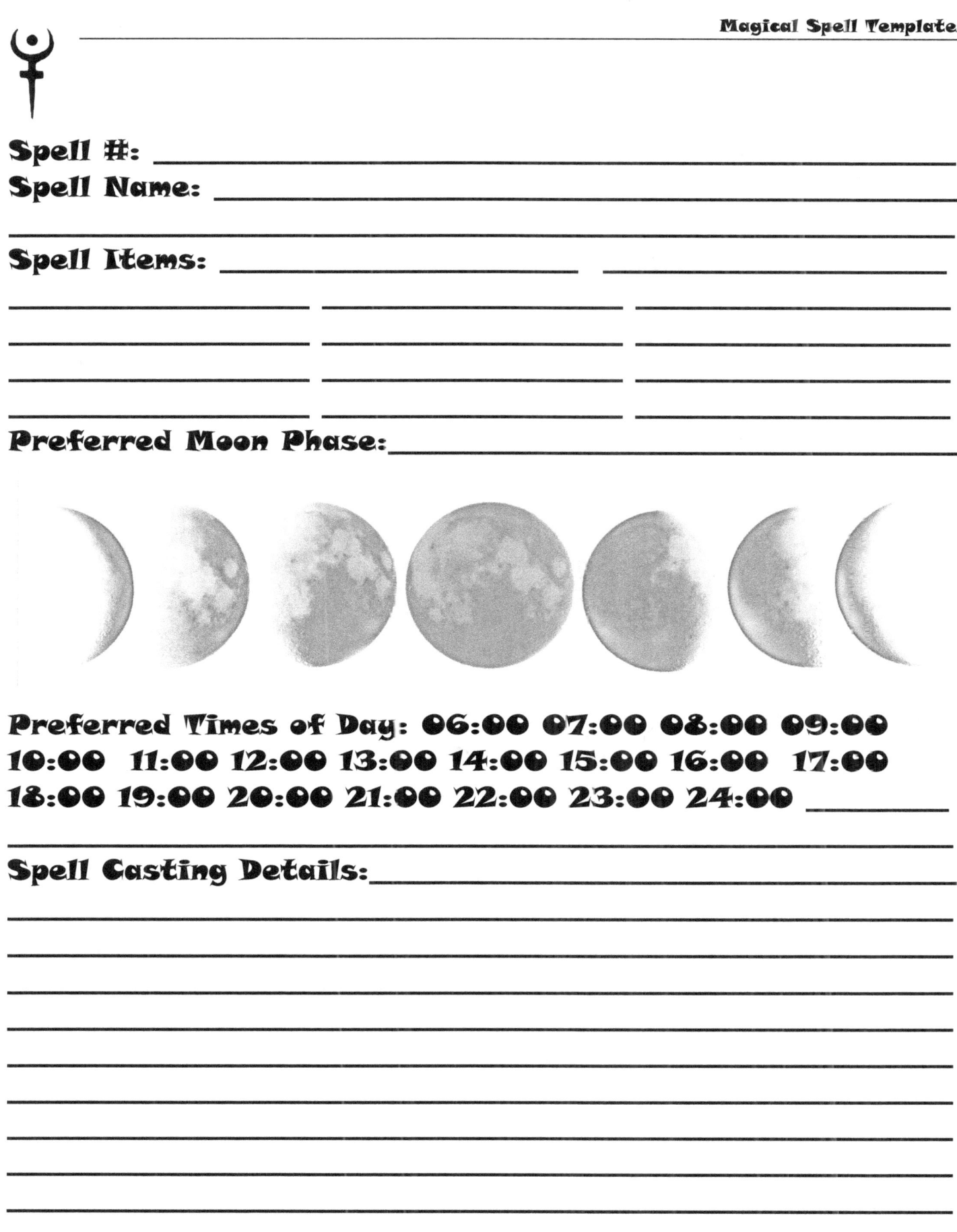

Spell #: _____

Spell Name: _____

_____

Spell Items: _____   _____

_____   _____   _____

_____   _____   _____

_____   _____   _____

_____   _____   _____

Preferred Moon Phase: _____

Preferred Times of Day: 06:00 07:00 08:00 09:00
10:00 11:00 12:00 13:00 14:00 15:00 16:00 17:00
18:00 19:00 20:00 21:00 22:00 23:00 24:00 _____

_____

Spell Casting Details: _____

_____

_____

_____

_____

_____

_____

_____

_____

_____

_____

Spell #: _____

Spell Name: _____

_____

Spell Items: _____ _____

_____ _____ _____

_____ _____ _____

_____ _____ _____

_____ _____ _____

Preferred Moon Phase: _____

**Preferred Times of Day: 06:00 07:00 08:00 09:00
10:00 11:00 12:00 13:00 14:00 15:00 16:00 17:00
18:00 19:00 20:00 21:00 22:00 23:00 24:00** _____

_____

Spell Casting Details: _____

_____

_____

_____

_____

_____

_____

_____

_____

_____

_____

Spell #: _____

Spell Name: _____

_____

Spell Items: _____   _____

_____   _____   _____

_____   _____   _____

_____   _____   _____

_____   _____   _____

Preferred Moon Phase: _____

Preferred Times of Day: 06:00 07:00 08:00 09:00 10:00 11:00 12:00 13:00 14:00 15:00 16:00 17:00 18:00 19:00 20:00 21:00 22:00 23:00 24:00 _____

Spell Casting Details: _____

_____

_____

_____

_____

_____

_____

_____

_____

_____

Spell #: _____

Spell Name: _____

_____

Spell Items: _____ _____

_____ _____ _____

_____ _____ _____

_____ _____ _____

_____ _____ _____

Preferred Moon Phase: _____

Preferred Times of Day: 06:00 07:00 08:00 09:00 10:00 11:00 12:00 13:00 14:00 15:00 16:00 17:00 18:00 19:00 20:00 21:00 22:00 23:00 24:00 _____

_____

Spell Casting Details: _____

_____

_____

_____

_____

_____

_____

_____

_____

_____

_____

Spell #: _____

Spell Name: _____

Spell Items: _____ _____

_____ _____ _____

_____ _____ _____

_____ _____ _____

_____ _____ _____

Preferred Moon Phase:_____

Preferred Times of Day: **06:00 07:00 08:00 09:00**
10:00 11:00 12:00 13:00 14:00 15:00 16:00 17:00
18:00 19:00 20:00 21:00 22:00 23:00 24:00 _____

Spell Casting Details:_____

_____

_____

_____

_____

_____

_____

_____

_____

_____

_____

Spell #: _____

Spell Name: _____
_____

Spell Items: _____ _____
_____ _____ _____
_____ _____ _____
_____ _____ _____
_____ _____ _____

Preferred Moon Phase:_____

Preferred Times of Day: **06:00 07:00 08:00 09:00 10:00 11:00 12:00 13:00 14:00 15:00 16:00 17:00 18:00 19:00 20:00 21:00 22:00 23:00 24:00** _____
_____

Spell Casting Details:_____
_____
_____
_____
_____
_____
_____
_____
_____
_____
_____

Spell #: _____

Spell Name: _____
_____

Spell Items: _____ _____
_____ _____ _____
_____ _____ _____
_____ _____ _____
_____ _____ _____

Preferred Moon Phase: _____

**Preferred Times of Day: 06:00 07:00 08:00 09:00
10:00 11:00 12:00 13:00 14:00 15:00 16:00 17:00
18:00 19:00 20:00 21:00 22:00 23:00 24:00 _____**

Spell Casting Details: _____
_____
_____
_____
_____
_____
_____
_____
_____
_____

Spell #: _____

Spell Name: _____

_____

Spell Items: _____ _____

_____ _____ _____

_____ _____ _____

_____ _____ _____

_____ _____ _____

Preferred Moon Phase: _____

Preferred Times of Day: 06:00 07:00 08:00 09:00
10:00 11:00 12:00 13:00 14:00 15:00 16:00 17:00
18:00 19:00 20:00 21:00 22:00 23:00 24:00 _____

_____

Spell Casting Details: _____

_____

_____

_____

_____

_____

_____

_____

_____

_____

_____

_____

Spell #: _____

Spell Name: _____

_____

Spell Items: _____   _____

_____   _____   _____

_____   _____   _____

_____   _____   _____

_____   _____   _____

Preferred Moon Phase: _____

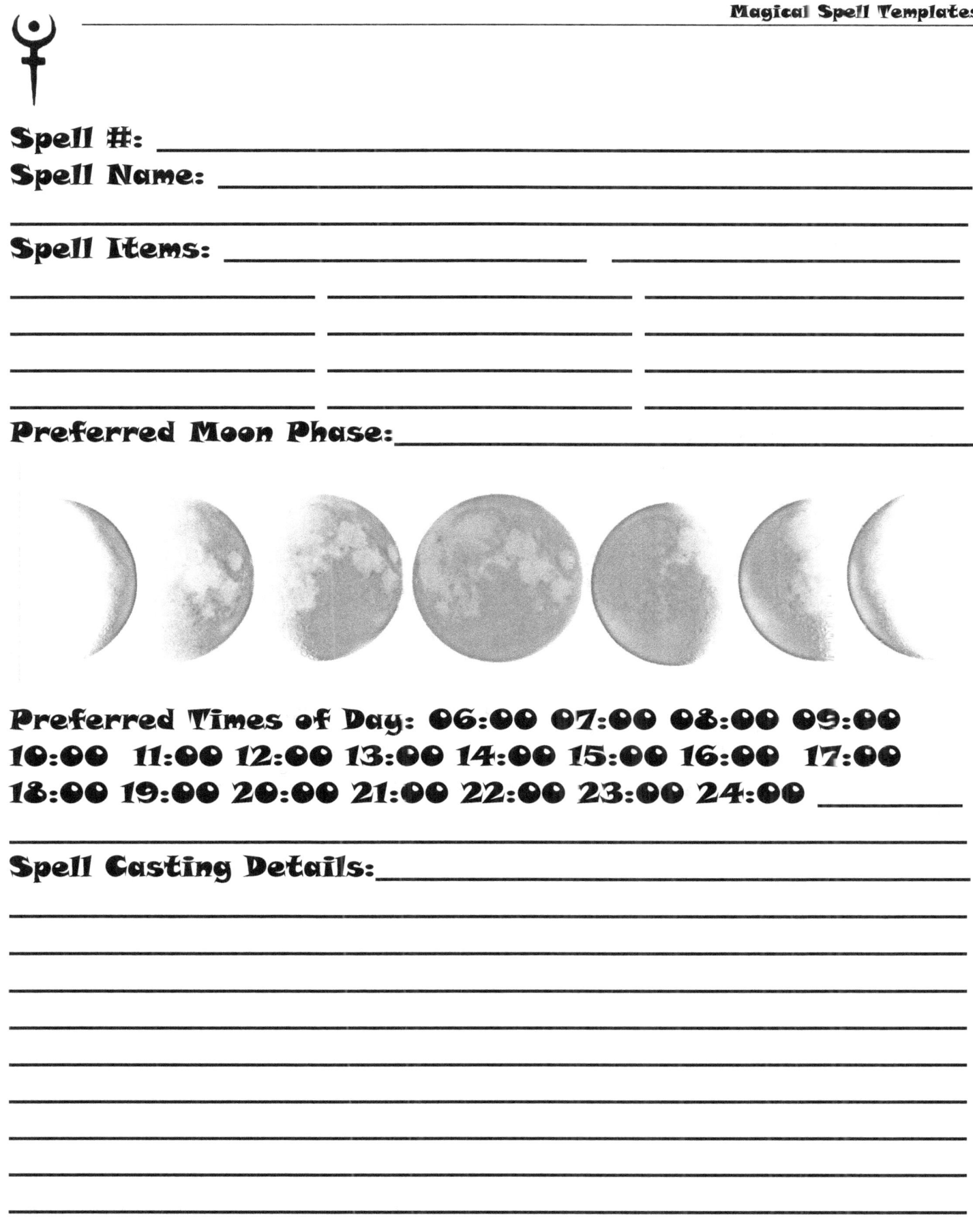

Preferred Times of Day: 06:00 07:00 08:00 09:00
10:00 11:00 12:00 13:00 14:00 15:00 16:00 17:00
18:00 19:00 20:00 21:00 22:00 23:00 24:00 _____

_____

Spell Casting Details: _____

_____

_____

_____

_____

_____

_____

_____

_____

_____

_____

_____

Spell #: _____

Spell Name: _____

_____

Spell Items: _____ _____

_____ _____ _____

_____ _____ _____

_____ _____ _____

_____ _____ _____

Preferred Moon Phase: _____

Preferred Times of Day: 06:00 07:00 08:00 09:00
10:00 11:00 12:00 13:00 14:00 15:00 16:00 17:00
18:00 19:00 20:00 21:00 22:00 23:00 24:00 _____

_____

Spell Casting Details: _____

_____

_____

_____

_____

_____

_____

_____

_____

_____

Spell #: _____

Spell Name: _____

_____

Spell Items: _____   _____

_____   _____   _____

_____   _____   _____

_____   _____   _____

_____   _____   _____

Preferred Moon Phase: _____

Preferred Times of Day: 06:00 07:00 08:00 09:00
10:00 11:00 12:00 13:00 14:00 15:00 16:00 17:00
18:00 19:00 20:00 21:00 22:00 23:00 24:00 _____

_____

Spell Casting Details: _____

_____

_____

_____

_____

_____

_____

_____

_____

_____

_____

Spell #: _____

Spell Name: _____

_____

Spell Items: _____ _____

_____ _____ _____

_____ _____ _____

_____ _____ _____

_____ _____ _____

Preferred Moon Phase:_____

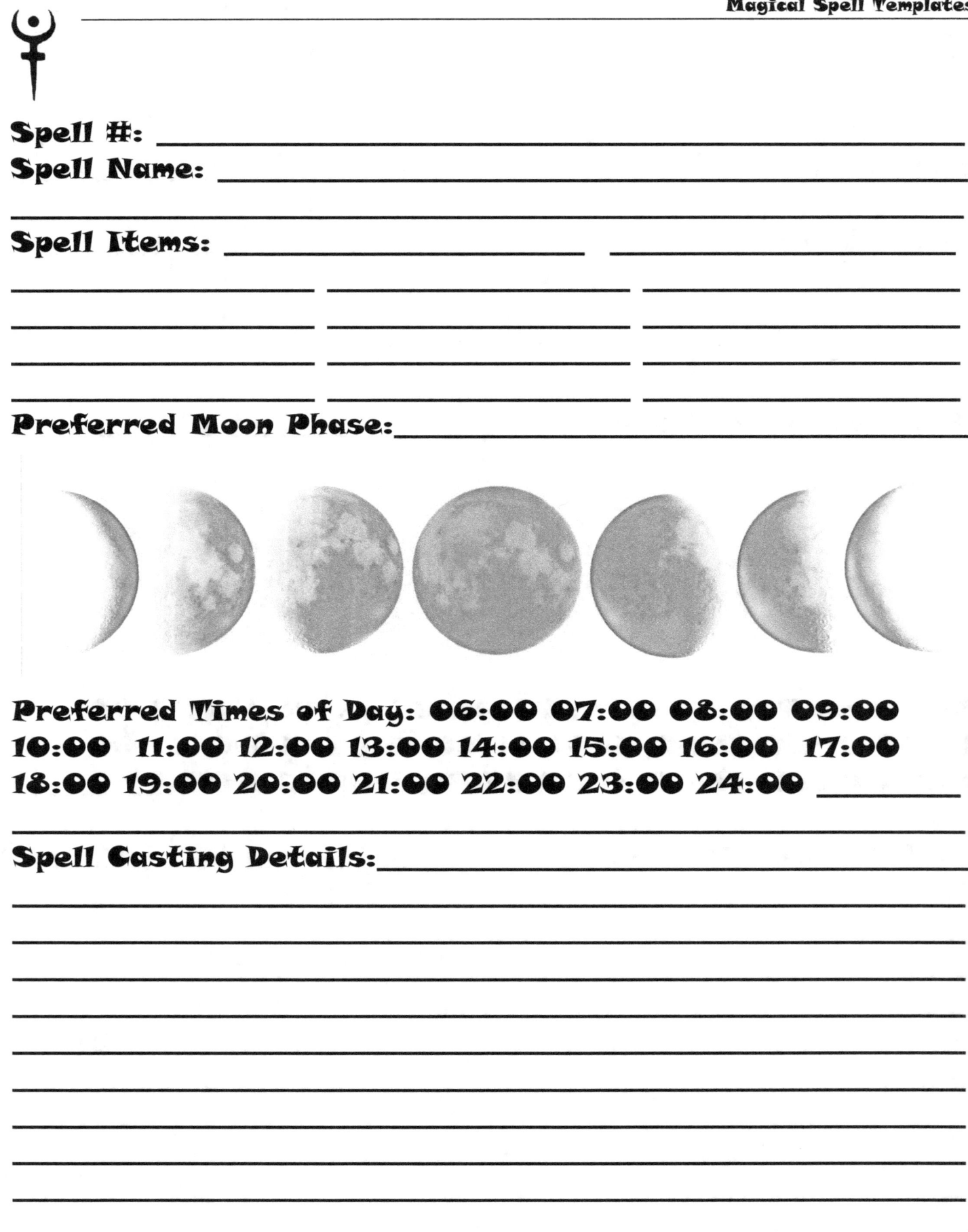

Preferred Times of Day: 06:00 07:00 08:00 09:00
10:00 11:00 12:00 13:00 14:00 15:00 16:00 17:00
18:00 19:00 20:00 21:00 22:00 23:00 24:00 _____

_____

Spell Casting Details:_____

_____

_____

_____

_____

_____

_____

_____

_____

_____

Spell #: _____

Spell Name: _____
_____

Spell Items: _____ _____
_____ _____
_____ _____
_____ _____
_____ _____

Preferred Moon Phase: _____

**Preferred Times of Day: 06:00 07:00 08:00 09:00
10:00 11:00 12:00 13:00 14:00 15:00 16:00 17:00
18:00 19:00 20:00 21:00 22:00 23:00 24:00 _____
_____**

Spell Casting Details: _____
_____
_____
_____
_____
_____
_____
_____
_____
_____
_____
_____
_____

Spell #: _____

Spell Name: _____

_____

Spell Items: _____ _____

_____ _____ _____

_____ _____ _____

_____ _____ _____

_____ _____ _____

Preferred Moon Phase:_____

Preferred Times of Day: 06:00 07:00 08:00 09:00
10:00 11:00 12:00 13:00 14:00 15:00 16:00 17:00
18:00 19:00 20:00 21:00 22:00 23:00 24:00 _____

_____

Spell Casting Details:_____

_____

_____

_____

_____

_____

_____

_____

_____

_____

_____

Spell #: _____

Spell Name: _____

_____

Spell Items: _____ _____

_____ _____ _____

_____ _____ _____

_____ _____ _____

Preferred Moon Phase: _____

Preferred Times of Day: 06:00 07:00 08:00 09:00
10:00 11:00 12:00 13:00 14:00 15:00 16:00 17:00
18:00 19:00 20:00 21:00 22:00 23:00 24:00 _____

_____

Spell Casting Details: _____

_____

_____

_____

_____

_____

_____

_____

_____

_____

_____

Spell #: _____

Spell Name: _____

_____

Spell Items: _____ _____

_____ _____ _____

_____ _____ _____

_____ _____ _____

_____ _____ _____

Preferred Moon Phase: _____

Preferred Times of Day: 06:00 07:00 08:00 09:00
10:00 11:00 12:00 13:00 14:00 15:00 16:00 17:00
18:00 19:00 20:00 21:00 22:00 23:00 24:00 _____

Spell Casting Details: _____

_____

_____

_____

_____

_____

_____

_____

_____

_____

Spell #: _____

Spell Name: _____

_____

Spell Items: _____ _____

_____ _____ _____

_____ _____ _____

_____ _____ _____

_____ _____ _____

Preferred Moon Phase: _____

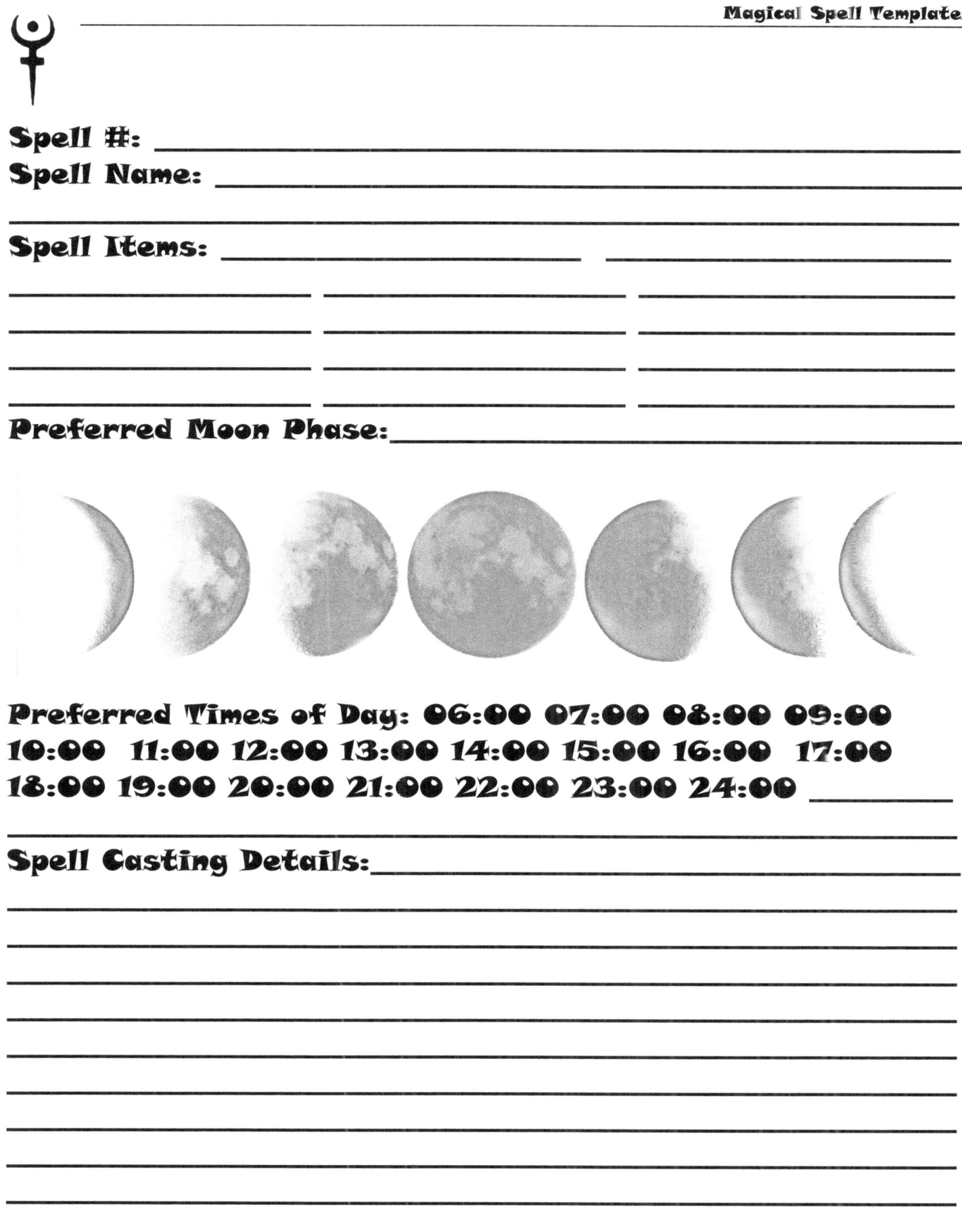

Preferred Times of Day: 06:00 07:00 08:00 09:00 10:00 11:00 12:00 13:00 14:00 15:00 16:00 17:00 18:00 19:00 20:00 21:00 22:00 23:00 24:00 _____

Spell Casting Details: _____

_____

_____

_____

_____

_____

_____

_____

_____

_____

_____

_____

Spell #: _____

Spell Name: _____

_____

Spell Items: _____ _____

_____ _____ _____

_____ _____ _____

_____ _____ _____

_____ _____ _____

Preferred Moon Phase:_____

**Preferred Times of Day: 06:00 07:00 08:00 09:00
10:00 11:00 12:00 13:00 14:00 15:00 16:00 17:00
18:00 19:00 20:00 21:00 22:00 23:00 24:00** _____

_____

Spell Casting Details:_____

_____

_____

_____

_____

_____

_____

_____

_____

_____

Spell #: _____

Spell Name: _____

_____

Spell Items: _____ _____

_____ _____ _____

_____ _____ _____

_____ _____ _____

_____ _____ _____

Preferred Moon Phase: _____

Preferred Times of Day: **06:00 07:00 08:00 09:00**
10:00 11:00 12:00 13:00 14:00 15:00 16:00 17:00
18:00 19:00 20:00 21:00 22:00 23:00 24:00 _____

Spell Casting Details: _____

_____

_____

_____

_____

_____

_____

_____

_____

_____

_____

Spell #: _____

Spell Name: _____

_____

Spell Items: _____ _____

_____ _____ _____

_____ _____ _____

_____ _____ _____

_____ _____ _____

Preferred Moon Phase: _____

**Preferred Times of Day: 06:00 07:00 08:00 09:00
10:00 11:00 12:00 13:00 14:00 15:00 16:00 17:00
18:00 19:00 20:00 21:00 22:00 23:00 24:00** _____

Spell Casting Details: _____

_____

_____

_____

_____

_____

_____

_____

_____

_____

Spell #: _____

Spell Name: _____

_____

Spell Items: _____ _____

_____ _____ _____

_____ _____ _____

_____ _____ _____

_____ _____ _____

Preferred Moon Phase: _____

Preferred Times of Day: **06:00 07:00 08:00 09:00**
10:00 11:00 12:00 13:00 14:00 15:00 16:00 17:00
18:00 19:00 20:00 21:00 22:00 23:00 24:00 _____

_____

Spell Casting Details: _____

_____

_____

_____

_____

_____

_____

_____

_____

_____

_____

_____

Spell #: _____

Spell Name: _____

_____

Spell Items: _____ _____

_____ _____ _____

_____ _____ _____

_____ _____ _____

_____ _____ _____

Preferred Moon Phase: _____

**Preferred Times of Day: 06:00 07:00 08:00 09:00
10:00 11:00 12:00 13:00 14:00 15:00 16:00 17:00
18:00 19:00 20:00 21:00 22:00 23:00 24:00** _____

_____

Spell Casting Details: _____

_____

_____

_____

_____

_____

_____

_____

_____

_____

Spell #: _____

Spell Name: _____

_____

Spell Items: _____ _____

_____ _____ _____

_____ _____ _____

_____ _____ _____

_____ _____ _____

Preferred Moon Phase: _____

**Preferred Times of Day: 06:00 07:00 08:00 09:00
10:00 11:00 12:00 13:00 14:00 15:00 16:00 17:00
18:00 19:00 20:00 21:00 22:00 23:00 24:00** _____

Spell Casting Details: _____

_____

_____

_____

_____

_____

_____

_____

_____

_____

_____

_____

Spell #: _____

Spell Name: _____

_____

Spell Items: _____ _____

_____ _____ _____

_____ _____ _____

_____ _____ _____

_____ _____ _____

Preferred Moon Phase:_____

Preferred Times of Day: 06:00 07:00 08:00 09:00
10:00 11:00 12:00 13:00 14:00 15:00 16:00 17:00
18:00 19:00 20:00 21:00 22:00 23:00 24:00 _____

_____

Spell Casting Details:_____

_____

_____

_____

_____

_____

_____

_____

_____

_____

_____

Spell #: _____

Spell Name: _____

_____

Spell Items: _____ _____

_____ _____ _____

_____ _____ _____

_____ _____ _____

_____ _____ _____

Preferred Moon Phase:_____

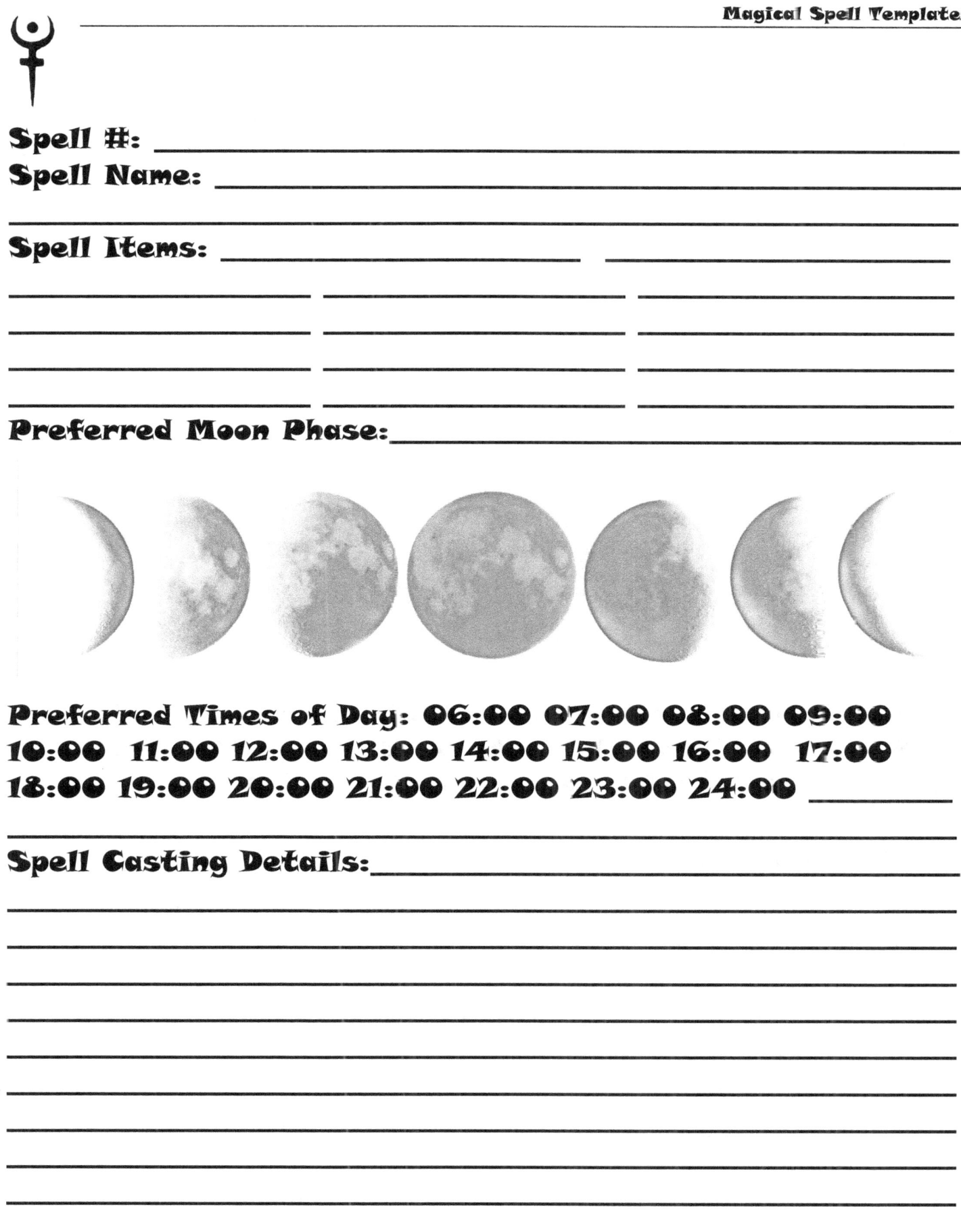

**Preferred Times of Day: 06:00 07:00 08:00 09:00
10:00 11:00 12:00 13:00 14:00 15:00 16:00 17:00
18:00 19:00 20:00 21:00 22:00 23:00 24:00** _____

_____

Spell Casting Details:_____

_____

_____

_____

_____

_____

_____

_____

_____

_____

_____

Spell #: _____

Spell Name: _____
_____

Spell Items: _____ _____
_____ _____ _____
_____ _____ _____
_____ _____ _____
_____ _____ _____

Preferred Moon Phase: _____

Preferred Times of Day: **06:00 07:00 08:00 09:00**
10:00 11:00 12:00 13:00 14:00 15:00 16:00 17:00
18:00 19:00 20:00 21:00 22:00 23:00 24:00 _____
_____

Spell Casting Details: _____
_____
_____
_____
_____
_____
_____
_____
_____
_____
_____

Spell #: _____

Spell Name: _____

_____

Spell Items: _____ _____

_____ _____ _____

_____ _____ _____

_____ _____ _____

_____ _____ _____

Preferred Moon Phase: _____

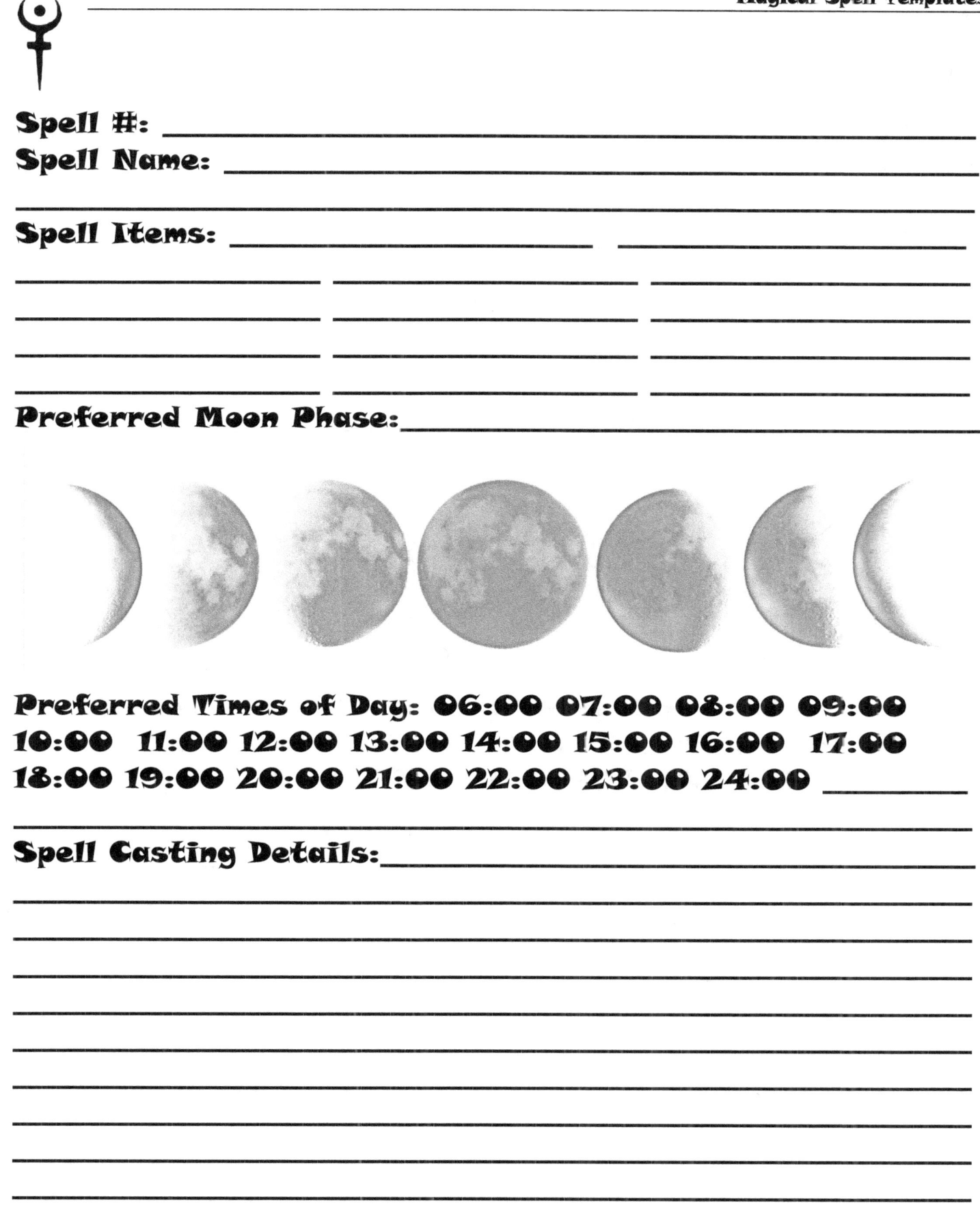

Preferred Times of Day: 06:00 07:00 08:00 09:00
10:00 11:00 12:00 13:00 14:00 15:00 16:00 17:00
18:00 19:00 20:00 21:00 22:00 23:00 24:00 _____

Spell Casting Details: _____

_____

_____

_____

_____

_____

_____

_____

_____

_____

_____

Spell #: _____

Spell Name: _____

_____

Spell Items: _____ _____

_____ _____ _____

_____ _____ _____

_____ _____ _____

_____ _____ _____

Preferred Moon Phase: _____

Preferred Times of Day: **06:00 07:00 08:00 09:00**
10:00 11:00 12:00 13:00 14:00 15:00 16:00 17:00
18:00 19:00 20:00 21:00 22:00 23:00 24:00 _____

_____

Spell Casting Details: _____

_____

_____

_____

_____

_____

_____

_____

_____

_____

_____

Spell #: _____
Spell Name: _____
_____

Spell Items: _____ _____
_____ _____
_____ _____
_____ _____
_____ _____

Preferred Moon Phase: _____

Preferred Times of Day: 06:00 07:00 08:00 09:00
10:00 11:00 12:00 13:00 14:00 15:00 16:00 17:00
18:00 19:00 20:00 21:00 22:00 23:00 24:00 _____

Spell Casting Details: _____
_____
_____
_____
_____
_____
_____
_____
_____
_____
_____
_____

Spell #: _____

Spell Name: _____
_____

Spell Items: _____ _____
_____ _____ _____
_____ _____ _____
_____ _____ _____
_____ _____ _____

Preferred Moon Phase: _____

**Preferred Times of Day: 06:00 07:00 08:00 09:00
10:00 11:00 12:00 13:00 14:00 15:00 16:00 17:00
18:00 19:00 20:00 21:00 22:00 23:00 24:00 _____**
_____

Spell Casting Details: _____
_____
_____
_____
_____
_____
_____
_____
_____
_____

Spell #: _____

Spell Name: _____
_____

Spell Items: _____   _____

_____   _____   _____

_____   _____   _____

_____   _____   _____

_____   _____   _____

Preferred Moon Phase:_____

Preferred Times of Day: **06:00 07:00 08:00 09:00 10:00 11:00 12:00 13:00 14:00 15:00 16:00 17:00 18:00 19:00 20:00 21:00 22:00 23:00 24:00** _____
_____

Spell Casting Details:_____
_____
_____
_____
_____
_____
_____
_____
_____
_____
_____

Spell #: _____

Spell Name: _____

_____

Spell Items: _____ _____

_____ _____ _____

_____ _____ _____

_____ _____ _____

_____ _____ _____

Preferred Moon Phase: _____

**Preferred Times of Day: 06:00 07:00 08:00 09:00
10:00 11:00 12:00 13:00 14:00 15:00 16:00 17:00
18:00 19:00 20:00 21:00 22:00 23:00 24:00** _____

_____

Spell Casting Details: _____

_____

_____

_____

_____

_____

_____

_____

_____

_____

Spell #: _____

Spell Name: _____

_____

Spell Items: _____   _____

_____   _____

_____   _____

_____   _____

_____   _____

Preferred Moon Phase: _____

Preferred Times of Day: 06:00 07:00 08:00 09:00
10:00 11:00 12:00 13:00 14:00 15:00 16:00 17:00
18:00 19:00 20:00 21:00 22:00 23:00 24:00 _____

_____

Spell Casting Details: _____

_____

_____

_____

_____

_____

_____

_____

_____

_____

_____

Spell #: _____

Spell Name: _____
_____

Spell Items: _____ _____
_____ _____ _____
_____ _____ _____
_____ _____ _____
_____ _____ _____

Preferred Moon Phase: _____

Preferred Times of Day: 06:00 07:00 08:00 09:00
10:00 11:00 12:00 13:00 14:00 15:00 16:00 17:00
18:00 19:00 20:00 21:00 22:00 23:00 24:00 _____
_____

Spell Casting Details: _____
_____
_____
_____
_____
_____
_____
_____
_____
_____
_____
_____

Spell #: _____

Spell Name: _____

Spell Items: _____ _____

_____ _____ _____

_____ _____ _____

_____ _____ _____

Preferred Moon Phase: _____

Preferred Times of Day: 06:00 07:00 08:00 09:00
10:00 11:00 12:00 13:00 14:00 15:00 16:00 17:00
18:00 19:00 20:00 21:00 22:00 23:00 24:00 _____

Spell Casting Details: _____

_____

_____

_____

_____

_____

_____

_____

_____

_____

Spell #: _____

Spell Name: _____

_____

Spell Items: _____ _____

_____ _____ _____

_____ _____ _____

_____ _____ _____

_____ _____ _____

Preferred Moon Phase: _____

Preferred Times of Day: 06:00 07:00 08:00 09:00
10:00 11:00 12:00 13:00 14:00 15:00 16:00 17:00
18:00 19:00 20:00 21:00 22:00 23:00 24:00 _____

Spell Casting Details: _____

_____

_____

_____

_____

_____

_____

_____

_____

_____

Spell #: _____

Spell Name: _____

_____

Spell Items: _____ _____

_____ _____ _____

_____ _____ _____

_____ _____ _____

_____ _____ _____

Preferred Moon Phase: _____

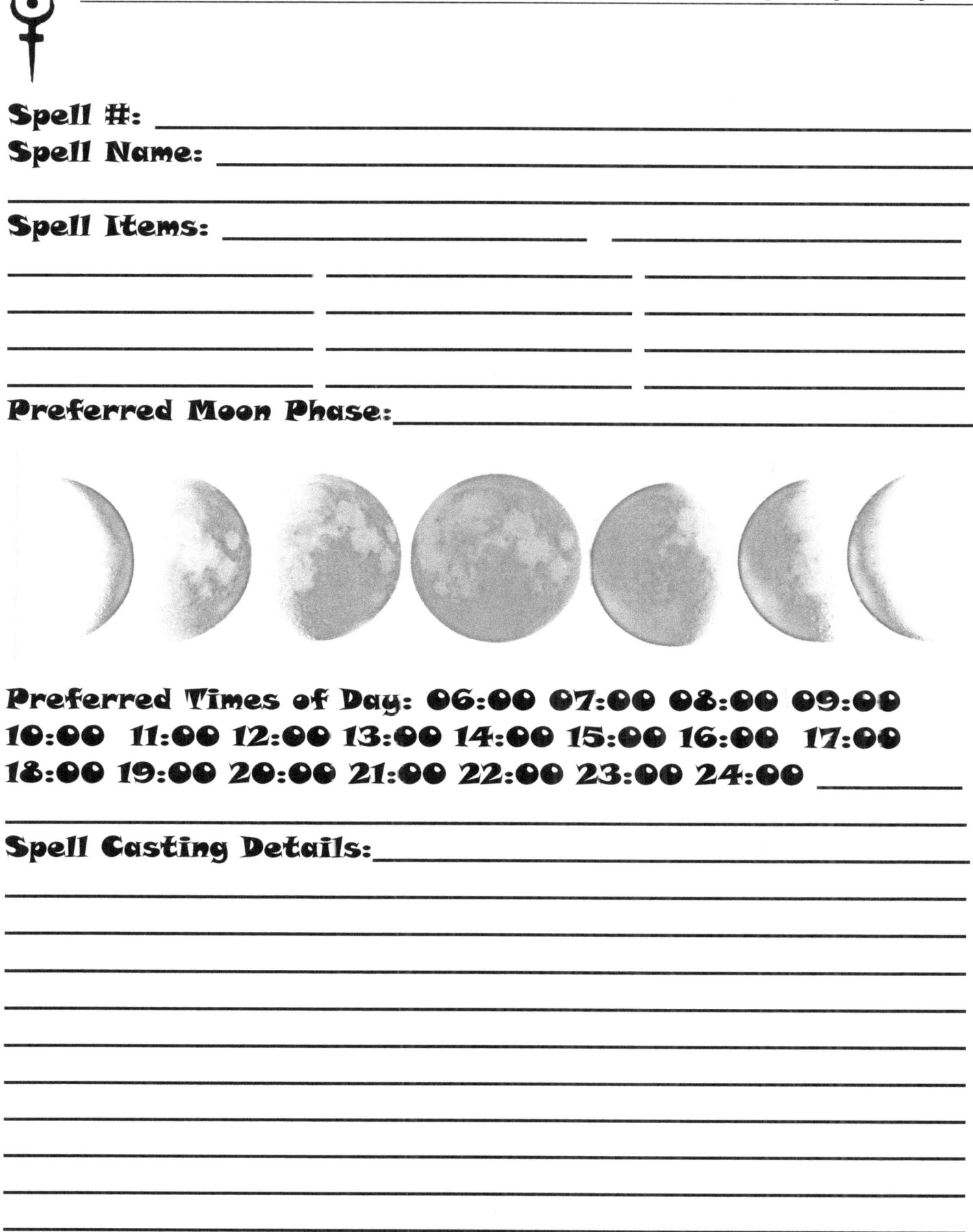

**Preferred Times of Day: 06:00 07:00 08:00 09:00
10:00 11:00 12:00 13:00 14:00 15:00 16:00 17:00
18:00 19:00 20:00 21:00 22:00 23:00 24:00** _____

_____

Spell Casting Details: _____

_____

_____

_____

_____

_____

_____

_____

_____

_____

_____

_____

Spell #: _____

Spell Name: _____

_____

Spell Items: _____ _____

_____ _____ _____

_____ _____ _____

_____ _____ _____

_____ _____ _____

Preferred Moon Phase:_____

Preferred Times of Day: 06:00 07:00 08:00 09:00
10:00 11:00 12:00 13:00 14:00 15:00 16:00 17:00
18:00 19:00 20:00 21:00 22:00 23:00 24:00 _____

_____

Spell Casting Details:_____

_____

_____

_____

_____

_____

_____

_____

_____

_____

_____

Spell #: _____

Spell Name: _____

_____

Spell Items: _____   _____

_____   _____   _____

_____   _____   _____

_____   _____   _____

_____   _____   _____

Preferred Moon Phase: _____

Preferred Times of Day: 06:00 07:00 08:00 09:00
10:00 11:00 12:00 13:00 14:00 15:00 16:00 17:00
18:00 19:00 20:00 21:00 22:00 23:00 24:00 _____

Spell Casting Details: _____

_____

_____

_____

_____

_____

_____

_____

_____

_____

Spell #: _____

Spell Name: _____

_____

Spell Items: _____ _____

_____ _____ _____

_____ _____ _____

_____ _____ _____

_____ _____ _____

Preferred Moon Phase:_____

Preferred Times of Day: 06:00 07:00 08:00 09:00
10:00 11:00 12:00 13:00 14:00 15:00 16:00 17:00
18:00 19:00 20:00 21:00 22:00 23:00 24:00 _____

_____

Spell Casting Details:_____

_____

_____

_____

_____

_____

_____

_____

_____

_____

Spell #: _____

Spell Name: _____
_____

Spell Items: _____ _____
_____ _____ _____
_____ _____ _____
_____ _____ _____
_____ _____ _____

Preferred Moon Phase: _____

**Preferred Times of Day: 06:00 07:00 08:00 09:00
10:00 11:00 12:00 13:00 14:00 15:00 16:00 17:00
18:00 19:00 20:00 21:00 22:00 23:00 24:00 _____**
_____

Spell Casting Details: _____
_____
_____
_____
_____
_____
_____
_____
_____
_____
_____
_____

Spell #: _____

Spell Name: _____
_____

Spell Items: _____ _____
_____ _____ _____
_____ _____ _____
_____ _____ _____
_____ _____ _____

Preferred Moon Phase: _____

Preferred Times of Day: 06:00 07:00 08:00 09:00
10:00 11:00 12:00 13:00 14:00 15:00 16:00 17:00
18:00 19:00 20:00 21:00 22:00 23:00 24:00 _____
_____

Spell Casting Details: _____
_____
_____
_____
_____
_____
_____
_____
_____
_____
_____

Spell #: _____

Spell Name: _____

_____

Spell Items: _____ _____

_____ _____ _____

_____ _____ _____

_____ _____ _____

Preferred Moon Phase: _____

Preferred Times of Day: 06:00 07:00 08:00 09:00
10:00 11:00 12:00 13:00 14:00 15:00 16:00 17:00
18:00 19:00 20:00 21:00 22:00 23:00 24:00 _____

_____

Spell Casting Details: _____

_____

_____

_____

_____

_____

_____

_____

_____

_____

_____

Spell #: _____

Spell Name: _____

_____

Spell Items: _____   _____

_____   _____   _____

_____   _____   _____

_____   _____   _____

_____   _____   _____

Preferred Moon Phase: _____

Preferred Times of Day: 06:00 07:00 08:00 09:00 10:00 11:00 12:00 13:00 14:00 15:00 16:00 17:00 18:00 19:00 20:00 21:00 22:00 23:00 24:00 _____

_____

Spell Casting Details: _____

_____

_____

_____

_____

_____

_____

_____

_____

_____

Spell #: _____

Spell Name: _____

Spell Items: _____ _____

_____ _____ _____

_____ _____ _____

_____ _____ _____

Preferred Moon Phase: _____

Preferred Times of Day: 06:00 07:00 08:00 09:00
10:00 11:00 12:00 13:00 14:00 15:00 16:00 17:00
18:00 19:00 20:00 21:00 22:00 23:00 24:00 _____

Spell Casting Details: _____

_____

_____

_____

_____

_____

_____

_____

_____

_____

_____

Spell #: _____

Spell Name: _____

_____

Spell Items: _____ _____

_____ _____

_____ _____

_____ _____

_____ _____

Preferred Moon Phase:_____

Preferred Times of Day: 06:00 07:00 08:00 09:00
10:00 11:00 12:00 13:00 14:00 15:00 16:00 17:00
18:00 19:00 20:00 21:00 22:00 23:00 24:00 _____

_____

Spell Casting Details:_____

_____

_____

_____

_____

_____

_____

_____

_____

_____

_____

Spell #: _____

Spell Name: _____

_____

Spell Items: _____ _____

_____ _____ _____

_____ _____ _____

_____ _____ _____

_____ _____ _____

Preferred Moon Phase: _____

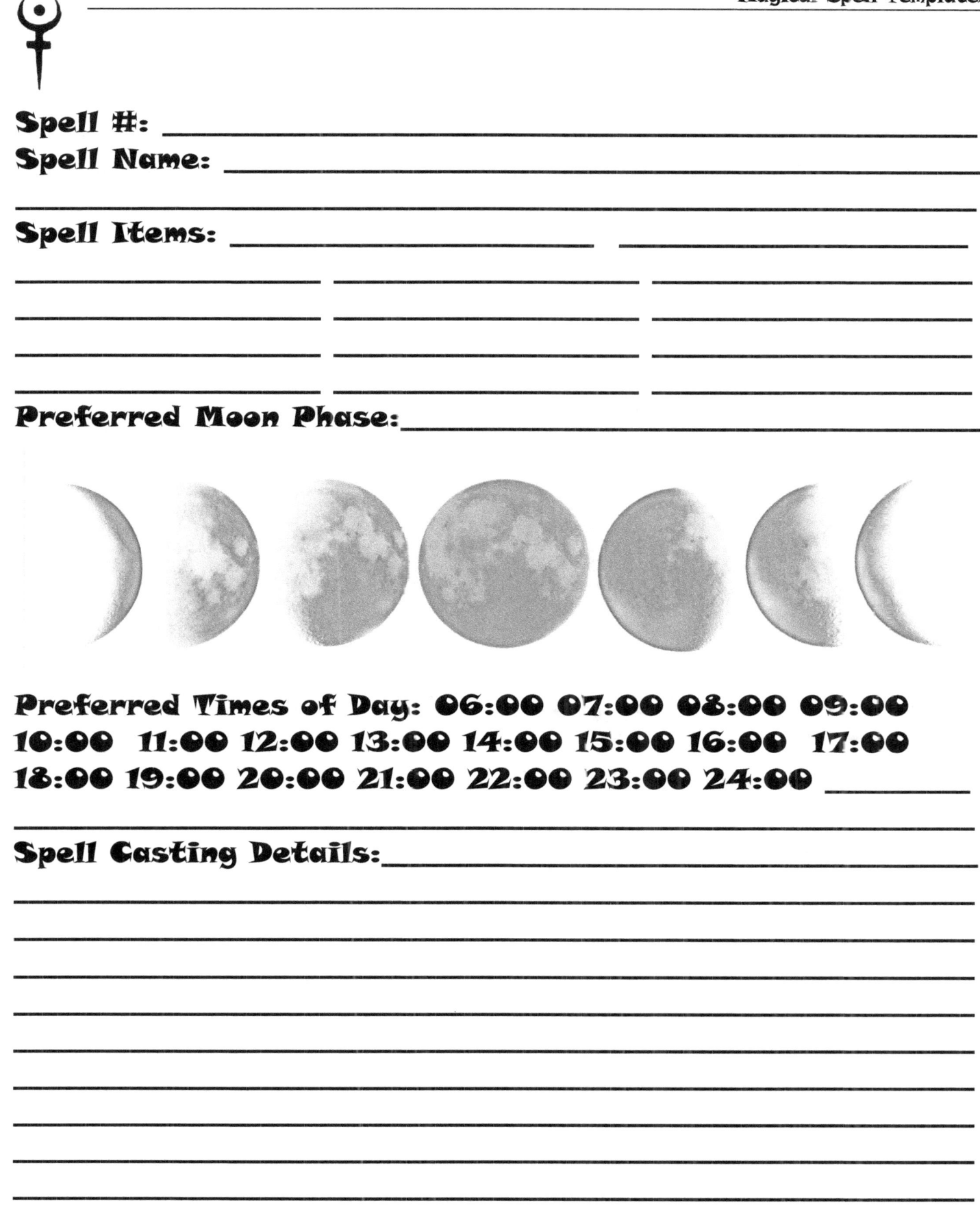

Preferred Times of Day: 06:00 07:00 08:00 09:00
10:00 11:00 12:00 13:00 14:00 15:00 16:00 17:00
18:00 19:00 20:00 21:00 22:00 23:00 24:00 _____

Spell Casting Details: _____

_____

_____

_____

_____

_____

_____

_____

_____

_____

_____

Spell #: _____

Spell Name: _____

_____

Spell Items: _____ _____

_____ _____

_____ _____

_____ _____

_____ _____

Preferred Moon Phase: _____

Preferred Times of Day: **06:00 07:00 08:00 09:00 10:00 11:00 12:00 13:00 14:00 15:00 16:00 17:00 18:00 19:00 20:00 21:00 22:00 23:00 24:00** _____

Spell Casting Details: _____

_____

_____

_____

_____

_____

_____

_____

_____

_____

_____

Spell #: _____

Spell Name: _____

_____

Spell Items: _____   _____

_____   _____

_____   _____

_____   _____

_____   _____

Preferred Moon Phase: _____

Preferred Times of Day: 06:00 07:00 08:00 09:00
10:00 11:00 12:00 13:00 14:00 15:00 16:00 17:00
18:00 19:00 20:00 21:00 22:00 23:00 24:00 _____

_____

Spell Casting Details: _____

_____

_____

_____

_____

_____

_____

_____

_____

_____

_____

_____

Spell #: _____

Spell Name: _____

_____

Spell Items: _____ _____

_____ _____

_____ _____

_____ _____

_____ _____

Preferred Moon Phase:_____

Preferred Times of Day: 06:00 07:00 08:00 09:00
10:00 11:00 12:00 13:00 14:00 15:00 16:00 17:00
18:00 19:00 20:00 21:00 22:00 23:00 24:00 _____

_____

Spell Casting Details:_____

_____

_____

_____

_____

_____

_____

_____

_____

_____

Spell #: _____

Spell Name: _____

_____

Spell Items: _____ _____

_____ _____ _____

_____ _____ _____

_____ _____ _____

_____ _____ _____

Preferred Moon Phase:_____

Preferred Times of Day: 06:00 07:00 08:00 09:00 10:00 11:00 12:00 13:00 14:00 15:00 16:00 17:00 18:00 19:00 20:00 21:00 22:00 23:00 24:00 _____

Spell Casting Details:_____

_____

_____

_____

_____

_____

_____

_____

_____

_____

_____

_____

Spell #: _____

Spell Name: _____

Spell Items: _____   _____

_____   _____   _____

_____   _____   _____

_____   _____   _____

_____   _____   _____

Preferred Moon Phase: _____

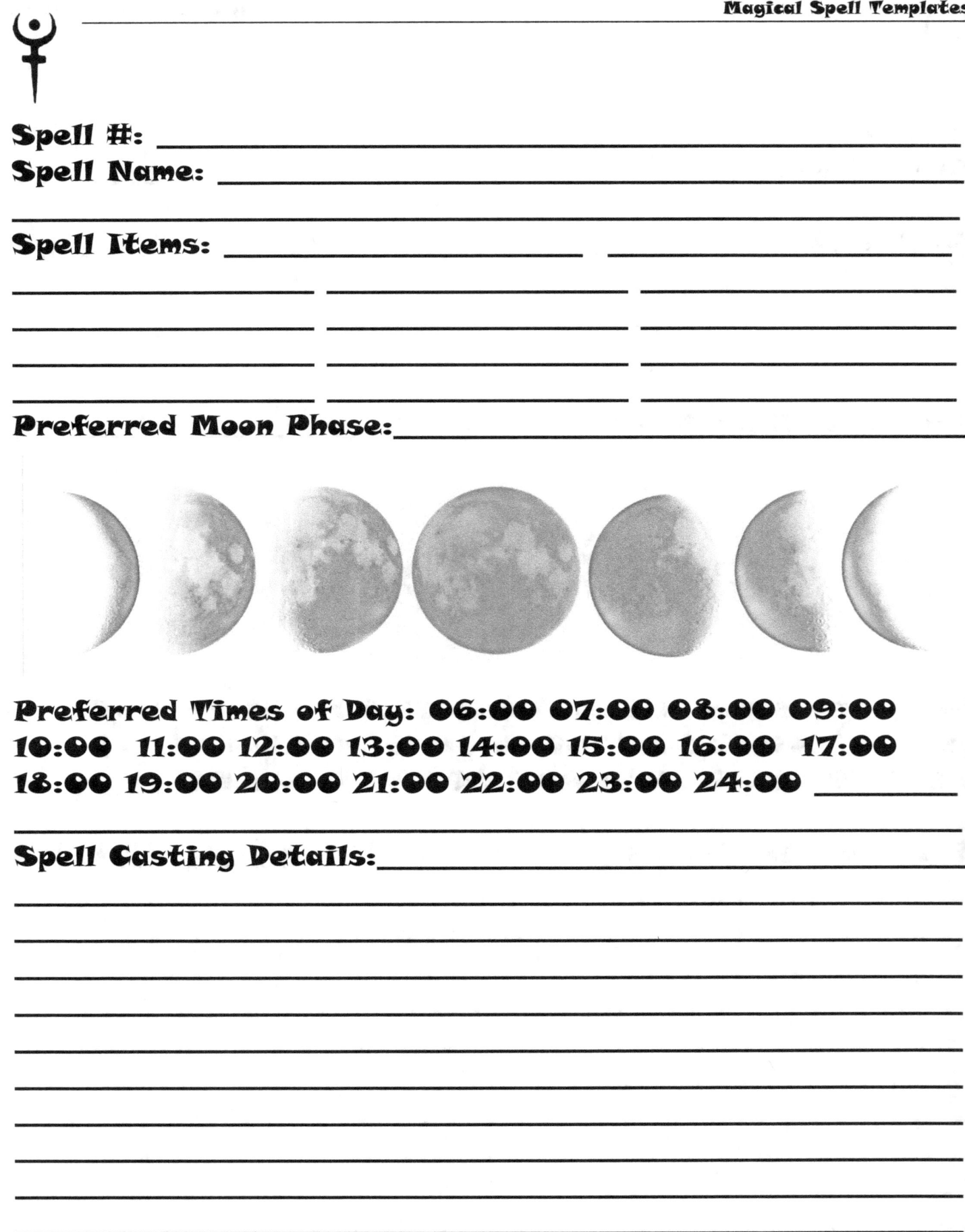

Preferred Times of Day: 06:00 07:00 08:00 09:00
10:00 11:00 12:00 13:00 14:00 15:00 16:00 17:00
18:00 19:00 20:00 21:00 22:00 23:00 24:00 _____

Spell Casting Details: _____

_____

_____

_____

_____

_____

_____

_____

_____

_____

Spell #: _____

Spell Name: _____

_____

Spell Items: _____ _____

_____ _____

_____ _____

_____ _____

_____ _____

Preferred Moon Phase: _____

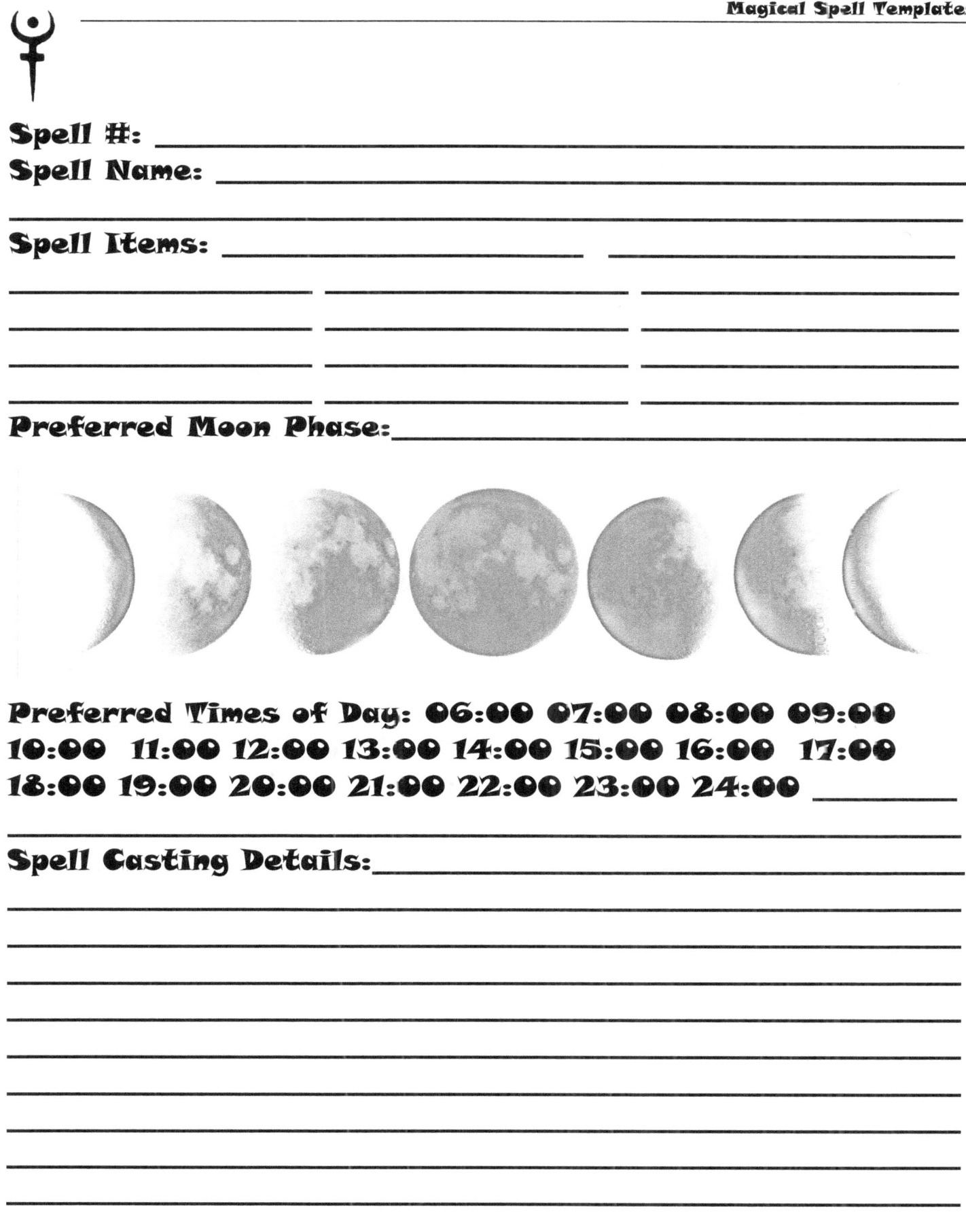

Preferred Times of Day: 06:00 07:00 08:00 09:00
10:00 11:00 12:00 13:00 14:00 15:00 16:00 17:00
18:00 19:00 20:00 21:00 22:00 23:00 24:00 _____

_____

Spell Casting Details: _____

_____

_____

_____

_____

_____

_____

_____

_____

_____

_____

Spell #: _____

Spell Name: _____

_____

Spell Items: _____ _____

_____ _____

_____ _____

_____ _____

_____ _____

Preferred Moon Phase:_____

Preferred Times of Day: 06:00 07:00 08:00 09:00 10:00 11:00 12:00 13:00 14:00 15:00 16:00 17:00 18:00 19:00 20:00 21:00 22:00 23:00 24:00 _____

_____

Spell Casting Details:_____

_____

_____

_____

_____

_____

_____

_____

_____

_____

_____

Spell #: _____

Spell Name: _____

_____

Spell Items: _____ _____

_____ _____ _____

_____ _____ _____

_____ _____ _____

Preferred Moon Phase: _____

Preferred Times of Day: 06:00 07:00 08:00 09:00
10:00 11:00 12:00 13:00 14:00 15:00 16:00 17:00
18:00 19:00 20:00 21:00 22:00 23:00 24:00 _____

_____

Spell Casting Details: _____

_____

_____

_____

_____

_____

_____

_____

_____

_____

Spell #: _____
Spell Name: _____
_____
Spell Items: _____   _____
_____   _____   _____
_____   _____   _____
_____   _____   _____
_____   _____   _____

Preferred Moon Phase: _____

Preferred Times of Day: **06:00 07:00 08:00 09:00 10:00 11:00 12:00 13:00 14:00 15:00 16:00 17:00 18:00 19:00 20:00 21:00 22:00 23:00 24:00** _____
_____

Spell Casting Details: _____
_____
_____
_____
_____
_____
_____
_____
_____
_____
_____

Spell #: _____

Spell Name: _____

_____

Spell Items: _____ _____

_____ _____ _____

_____ _____ _____

_____ _____ _____

_____ _____ _____

Preferred Moon Phase: _____

Preferred Times of Day: 06:00 07:00 08:00 09:00
10:00 11:00 12:00 13:00 14:00 15:00 16:00 17:00
18:00 19:00 20:00 21:00 22:00 23:00 24:00 _____

_____

Spell Casting Details: _____

_____

_____

_____

_____

_____

_____

_____

_____

_____

_____

_____

Spell #: _____

Spell Name: _____
_____

Spell Items: _____ _____
_____ _____
_____ _____
_____ _____
_____ _____

Preferred Moon Phase:_____

Preferred Times of Day: 06:00 07:00 08:00 09:00
10:00 11:00 12:00 13:00 14:00 15:00 16:00 17:00
18:00 19:00 20:00 21:00 22:00 23:00 24:00 _____
_____

Spell Casting Details:_____
_____
_____
_____
_____
_____
_____
_____
_____
_____
_____
_____

Spell #: _____

Spell Name: _____

_____

Spell Items: _____ _____

_____ _____ _____

_____ _____ _____

_____ _____ _____

_____ _____ _____

Preferred Moon Phase: _____

**Preferred Times of Day: 06:00 07:00 08:00 09:00
10:00 11:00 12:00 13:00 14:00 15:00 16:00 17:00
18:00 19:00 20:00 21:00 22:00 23:00 24:00 _____**

Spell Casting Details: _____

_____

_____

_____

_____

_____

_____

_____

_____

_____

_____

Spell #: _____

Spell Name: _____

_____

Spell Items: _____ _____

_____ _____

_____ _____

_____ _____

_____ _____

Preferred Moon Phase:_____

**Preferred Times of Day: 06:00 07:00 08:00 09:00
10:00 11:00 12:00 13:00 14:00 15:00 16:00 17:00
18:00 19:00 20:00 21:00 22:00 23:00 24:00 _____**

_____

Spell Casting Details:_____

_____

_____

_____

_____

_____

_____

_____

_____

_____

_____

Spell #: _____

Spell Name: _____
_____

Spell Items: _____ _____
_____ _____ _____
_____ _____ _____
_____ _____ _____
_____ _____ _____

Preferred Moon Phase: _____

**Preferred Times of Day: 06:00 07:00 08:00 09:00
10:00 11:00 12:00 13:00 14:00 15:00 16:00 17:00
18:00 19:00 20:00 21:00 22:00 23:00 24:00 _____**
_____

Spell Casting Details: _____
_____
_____
_____
_____
_____
_____
_____
_____
_____
_____
_____

Spell #: _____

Spell Name: _____
_____

Spell Items: _____ _____

_____ _____

_____ _____

_____ _____

_____ _____

Preferred Moon Phase:_____

Preferred Times of Day: 06:00 07:00 08:00 09:00
10:00 11:00 12:00 13:00 14:00 15:00 16:00 17:00
18:00 19:00 20:00 21:00 22:00 23:00 24:00 _____
_____

Spell Casting Details:_____
_____
_____
_____
_____
_____
_____
_____
_____
_____
_____

Spell #: _____

Spell Name: _____
_____

Spell Items: _____ _____

_____ _____ _____

_____ _____ _____

_____ _____ _____

_____ _____ _____

Preferred Moon Phase: _____

Preferred Times of Day: 06:00 07:00 08:00 09:00
10:00 11:00 12:00 13:00 14:00 15:00 16:00 17:00
18:00 19:00 20:00 21:00 22:00 23:00 24:00 _____

Spell Casting Details: _____

_____

_____

_____

_____

_____

_____

_____

_____

_____

_____

Spell #: _____

Spell Name: _____

_____

Spell Items: _____ _____

_____ _____

_____ _____

_____ _____

_____ _____

Preferred Moon Phase: _____

Preferred Times of Day: 06:00 07:00 08:00 09:00
10:00 11:00 12:00 13:00 14:00 15:00 16:00 17:00
18:00 19:00 20:00 21:00 22:00 23:00 24:00 _____

Spell Casting Details: _____

_____

_____

_____

_____

_____

_____

_____

_____

_____

Spell #: _____

Spell Name: _____

_____

Spell Items: _____ _____

_____ _____ _____

_____ _____ _____

_____ _____ _____

_____ _____ _____

Preferred Moon Phase:_____

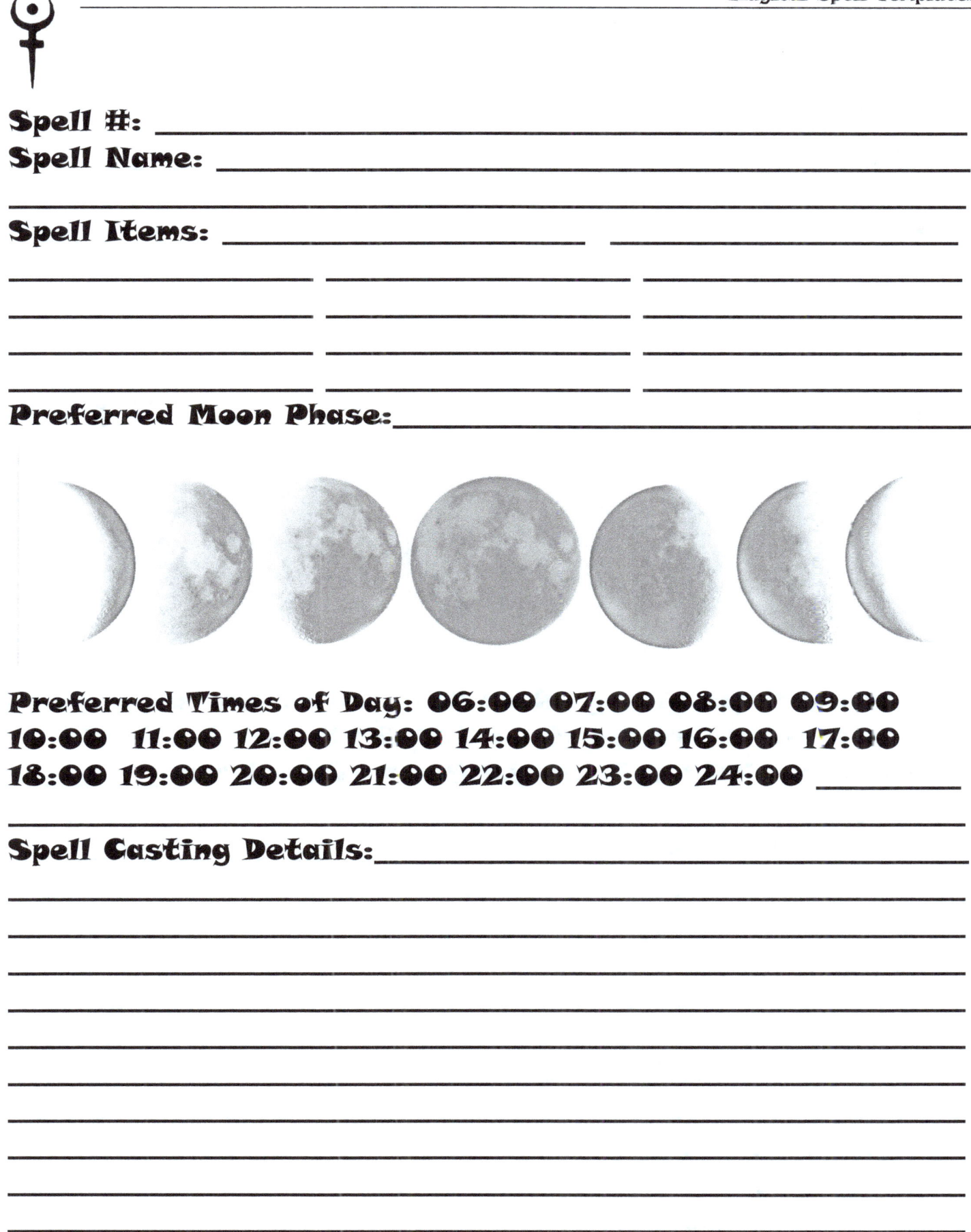

Preferred Times of Day: 06:00 07:00 08:00 09:00
10:00 11:00 12:00 13:00 14:00 15:00 16:00 17:00
18:00 19:00 20:00 21:00 22:00 23:00 24:00 _____

_____

Spell Casting Details:_____

_____

_____

_____

_____

_____

_____

_____

_____

_____

_____

Spell #: _____

Spell Name: _____
_____

Spell Items: _____ _____
_____ _____
_____ _____
_____ _____
_____ _____

Preferred Moon Phase:_____

Preferred Times of Day: 06:00 07:00 08:00 09:00
10:00 11:00 12:00 13:00 14:00 15:00 16:00 17:00
18:00 19:00 20:00 21:00 22:00 23:00 24:00 _____
_____

Spell Casting Details:_____
_____
_____
_____
_____
_____
_____
_____
_____
_____
_____

Spell #: _____

Spell Name: _____

_____

Spell Items: _____ _____

_____ _____ _____

_____ _____ _____

_____ _____ _____

_____ _____ _____

Preferred Moon Phase:_____

Preferred Times of Day: 06:00 07:00 08:00 09:00
10:00 11:00 12:00 13:00 14:00 15:00 16:00 17:00
18:00 19:00 20:00 21:00 22:00 23:00 24:00 _____

Spell Casting Details:_____

_____

_____

_____

_____

_____

_____

_____

_____

_____

_____

Spell #: _____

Spell Name: _____

_____

Spell Items: _____ _____

_____ _____

_____ _____

_____ _____

_____ _____

Preferred Moon Phase: _____

Preferred Times of Day: 06:00 07:00 08:00 09:00
10:00 11:00 12:00 13:00 14:00 15:00 16:00 17:00
18:00 19:00 20:00 21:00 22:00 23:00 24:00 _____

_____

Spell Casting Details: _____

_____

_____

_____

_____

_____

_____

_____

_____

_____

_____

Spell #: _____

Spell Name: _____

_____

Spell Items: _____ _____

_____ _____ _____

_____ _____ _____

_____ _____ _____

_____ _____ _____

Preferred Moon Phase: _____

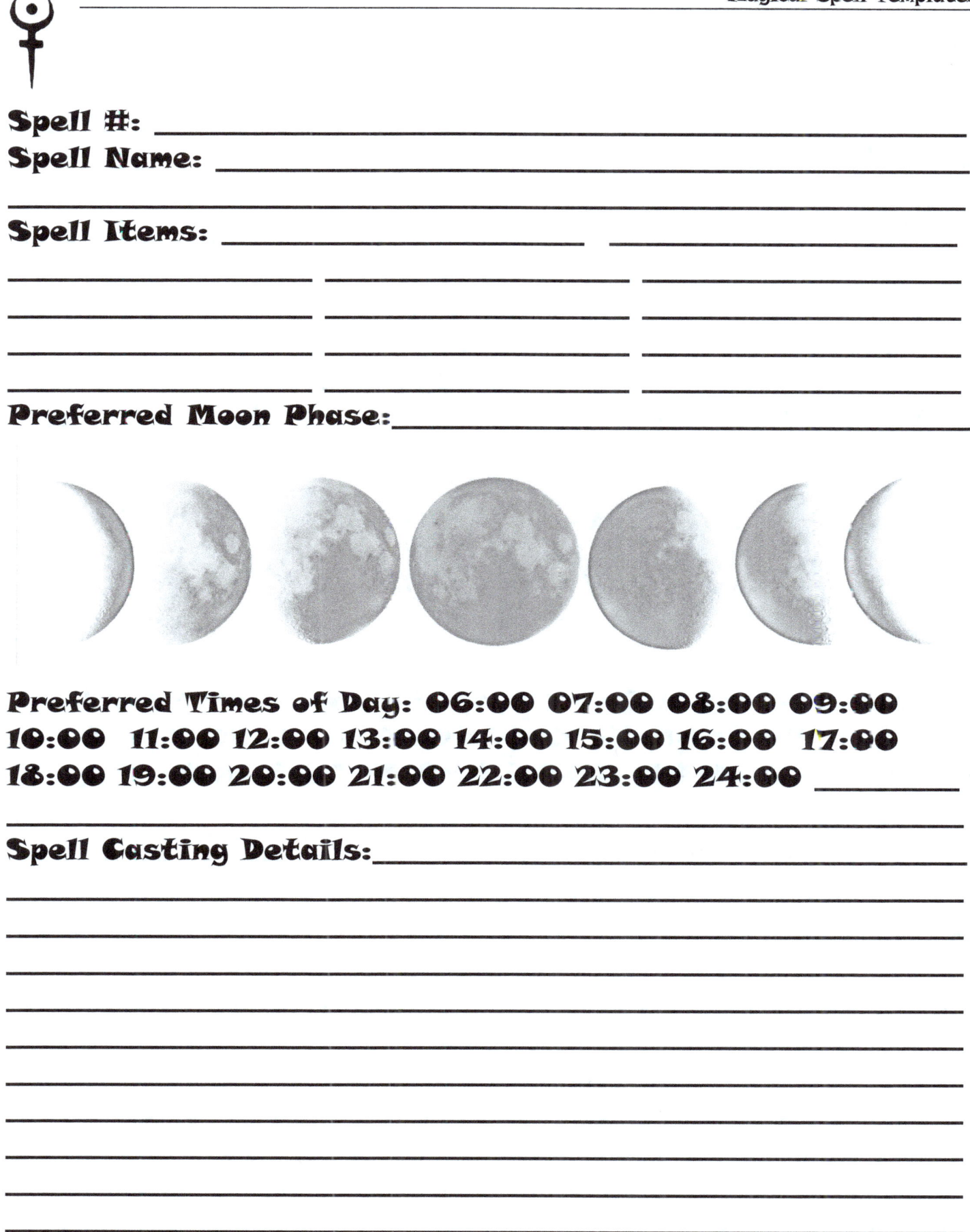

Preferred Times of Day: 06:00 07:00 08:00 09:00
10:00 11:00 12:00 13:00 14:00 15:00 16:00 17:00
18:00 19:00 20:00 21:00 22:00 23:00 24:00 _____

Spell Casting Details: _____

_____

_____

_____

_____

_____

_____

_____

_____

_____

_____

Spell #: _____

Spell Name: _____

_____

Spell Items: _____ _____

_____ _____ _____

_____ _____ _____

_____ _____ _____

_____ _____ _____

Preferred Moon Phase: _____

Preferred Times of Day: 06:00 07:00 08:00 09:00
10:00 11:00 12:00 13:00 14:00 15:00 16:00 17:00
18:00 19:00 20:00 21:00 22:00 23:00 24:00 _____

_____

Spell Casting Details: _____

_____

_____

_____

_____

_____

_____

_____

_____

_____

Spell #: _____

Spell Name: _____

_____

Spell Items: _____ _____

_____ _____ _____

_____ _____ _____

_____ _____ _____

_____ _____ _____

Preferred Moon Phase: _____

Preferred Times of Day: **06:00 07:00 08:00 09:00 10:00 11:00 12:00 13:00 14:00 15:00 16:00 17:00 18:00 19:00 20:00 21:00 22:00 23:00 24:00** _____

Spell Casting Details: _____

_____

_____

_____

_____

_____

_____

_____

_____

_____

_____

_____

Spell #: _____

Spell Name: _____

_____

Spell Items: _____ _____

_____ _____

_____ _____

_____ _____

Preferred Moon Phase: _____

Preferred Times of Day: 06:00 07:00 08:00 09:00
10:00 11:00 12:00 13:00 14:00 15:00 16:00 17:00
18:00 19:00 20:00 21:00 22:00 23:00 24:00 _____

_____

Spell Casting Details: _____

_____

_____

_____

_____

_____

_____

_____

_____

_____

_____

Spell #: _____

Spell Name: _____

_____

Spell Items: _____ _____

_____ _____

_____ _____

_____ _____

_____ _____

Preferred Moon Phase:_____

**Preferred Times of Day: 06:00 07:00 08:00 09:00
10:00 11:00 12:00 13:00 14:00 15:00 16:00 17:00
18:00 19:00 20:00 21:00 22:00 23:00 24:00 _____**

_____

Spell Casting Details:_____

_____

_____

_____

_____

_____

_____

_____

_____

_____

_____

Spell #: _____

Spell Name: _____
_____

Spell Items: _____ _____
_____ _____ _____
_____ _____ _____
_____ _____ _____
_____ _____ _____

Preferred Moon Phase:_____

Preferred Times of Day: 06:00 07:00 08:00 09:00
10:00 11:00 12:00 13:00 14:00 15:00 16:00 17:00
18:00 19:00 20:00 21:00 22:00 23:00 24:00 _____
_____

Spell Casting Details:_____
_____
_____
_____
_____
_____
_____
_____
_____
_____
_____

Spell #: _____

Spell Name: _____
_____

Spell Items: _____ _____
_____ _____ _____
_____ _____ _____
_____ _____ _____
_____ _____ _____

Preferred Moon Phase: _____

Preferred Times of Day: **06:00 07:00 08:00 09:00**
10:00 11:00 12:00 13:00 14:00 15:00 16:00 17:00
18:00 19:00 20:00 21:00 22:00 23:00 24:00 _____

Spell Casting Details: _____
_____
_____
_____
_____
_____
_____
_____
_____
_____

Spell #: _____
Spell Name: _____
_____
Spell Items: _____ _____
_____ _____ _____
_____ _____ _____
_____ _____ _____
_____ _____ _____

Preferred Moon Phase:_____

Preferred Times of Day: 06:00 07:00 08:00 09:00
10:00 11:00 12:00 13:00 14:00 15:00 16:00 17:00
18:00 19:00 20:00 21:00 22:00 23:00 24:00 _____
_____

Spell Casting Details:_____
_____
_____
_____
_____
_____
_____
_____
_____
_____
_____

Spell #: _____

Spell Name: _____

_____

Spell Items: _____ _____

_____ _____ _____

_____ _____ _____

_____ _____ _____

_____ _____ _____

Preferred Moon Phase: _____

Preferred Times of Day: 06:00 07:00 08:00 09:00
10:00 11:00 12:00 13:00 14:00 15:00 16:00 17:00
18:00 19:00 20:00 21:00 22:00 23:00 24:00 _____

Spell Casting Details: _____

_____

_____

_____

_____

_____

_____

_____

_____

_____

_____

Spell #: _____

Spell Name: _____
_____

Spell Items: _____   _____
_____   _____   _____
_____   _____   _____
_____   _____   _____
_____   _____   _____

Preferred Moon Phase:_____

Preferred Times of Day: 06:00 07:00 08:00 09:00
10:00 11:00 12:00 13:00 14:00 15:00 16:00 17:00
18:00 19:00 20:00 21:00 22:00 23:00 24:00 _____
_____

Spell Casting Details:_____
_____
_____
_____
_____
_____
_____
_____
_____
_____
_____

Spell #: _____

Spell Name: _____
_____

Spell Items: _____ _____
_____ _____ _____
_____ _____ _____
_____ _____ _____
_____ _____ _____

Preferred Moon Phase: _____

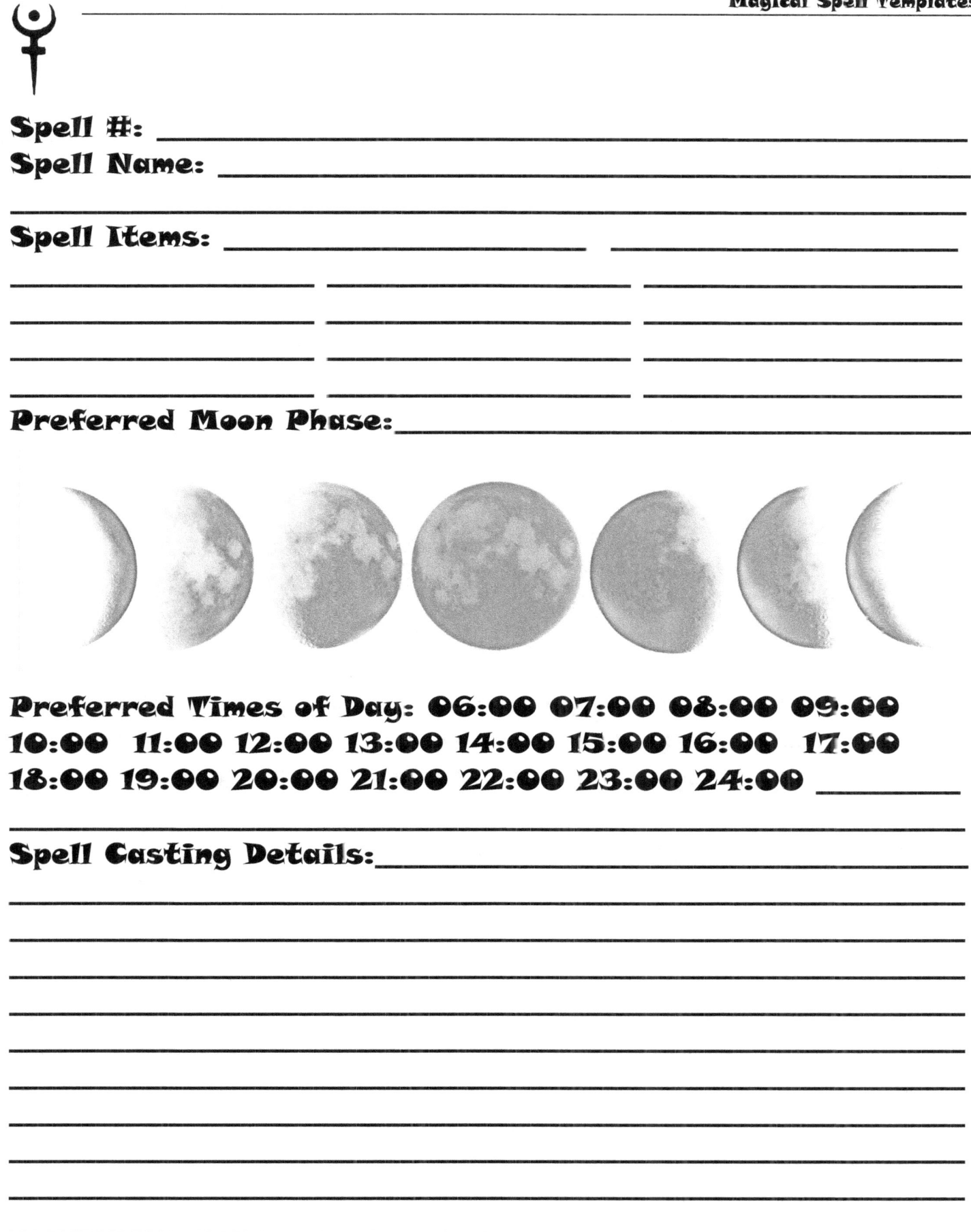

Preferred Times of Day: 06:00 07:00 08:00 09:00
10:00 11:00 12:00 13:00 14:00 15:00 16:00 17:00
18:00 19:00 20:00 21:00 22:00 23:00 24:00 _____

Spell Casting Details: _____
_____
_____
_____
_____
_____
_____
_____
_____
_____
_____

Spell #: _____

Spell Name: _____

_____

Spell Items: _____   _____

_____   _____

_____   _____

_____   _____

_____   _____

Preferred Moon Phase: _____

Preferred Times of Day: **06:00 07:00 08:00 09:00 10:00 11:00 12:00 13:00 14:00 15:00 16:00 17:00 18:00 19:00 20:00 21:00 22:00 23:00 24:00** _____

_____

Spell Casting Details: _____

_____

_____

_____

_____

_____

_____

_____

_____

_____

Spell #: _____

Spell Name: _____

_____

Spell Items: _____ _____

_____ _____ _____

_____ _____ _____

_____ _____ _____

_____ _____ _____

Preferred Moon Phase: _____

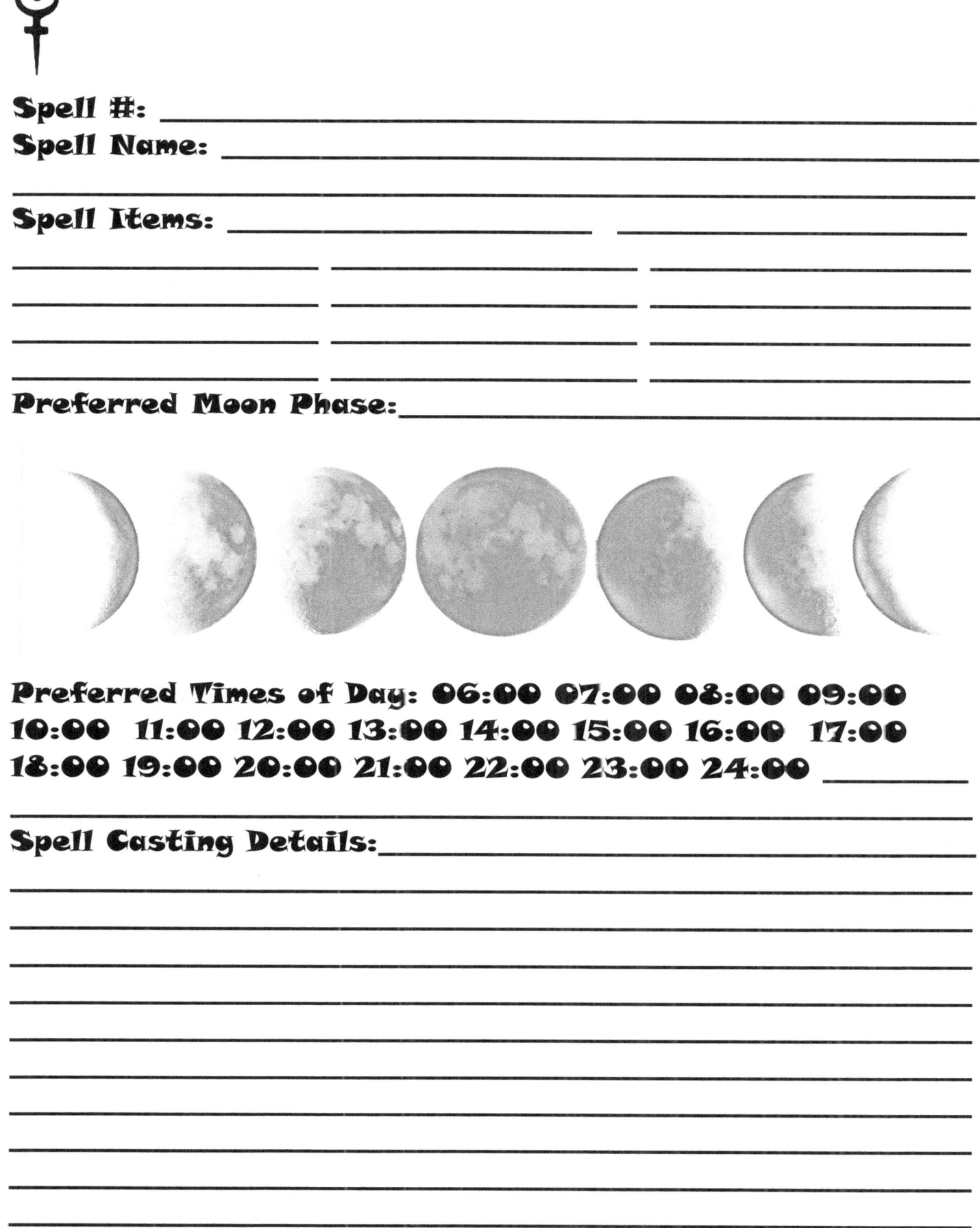

**Preferred Times of Day: 06:00 07:00 08:00 09:00
10:00 11:00 12:00 13:00 14:00 15:00 16:00 17:00
18:00 19:00 20:00 21:00 22:00 23:00 24:00** _____

Spell Casting Details: _____

_____

_____

_____

_____

_____

_____

_____

_____

_____

_____

Spell #: _____

Spell Name: _____

_____

Spell Items: _____ _____

_____ _____ _____

_____ _____ _____

_____ _____ _____

_____ _____ _____

Preferred Moon Phase:_____

**Preferred Times of Day: 06:00 07:00 08:00 09:00
10:00 11:00 12:00 13:00 14:00 15:00 16:00 17:00
18:00 19:00 20:00 21:00 22:00 23:00 24:00** _____

_____

Spell Casting Details:_____

_____

_____

_____

_____

_____

_____

_____

_____

_____

Spell #: _____

Spell Name: _____

_____

Spell Items: _____ _____

_____ _____ _____

_____ _____ _____

_____ _____ _____

_____ _____ _____

Preferred Moon Phase: _____

Preferred Times of Day: 06:00 07:00 08:00 09:00
10:00 11:00 12:00 13:00 14:00 15:00 16:00 17:00
18:00 19:00 20:00 21:00 22:00 23:00 24:00 _____

Spell Casting Details: _____

_____

_____

_____

_____

_____

_____

_____

_____

_____

_____

Spell #: _____

Spell Name: _____

_____

Spell Items: _____ _____

_____ _____

_____ _____

_____ _____

_____ _____

Preferred Moon Phase:_____

Preferred Times of Day: 06:00 07:00 08:00 09:00
10:00 11:00 12:00 13:00 14:00 15:00 16:00 17:00
18:00 19:00 20:00 21:00 22:00 23:00 24:00 _____

_____

Spell Casting Details:_____

_____

_____

_____

_____

_____

_____

_____

_____

_____

Spell #: _____

Spell Name: _____

_____

Spell Items: _____ _____

_____ _____ _____

_____ _____ _____

_____ _____ _____

_____ _____ _____

Preferred Moon Phase: _____

Preferred Times of Day: 06:00 07:00 08:00 09:00 10:00 11:00 12:00 13:00 14:00 15:00 16:00 17:00 18:00 19:00 20:00 21:00 22:00 23:00 24:00 _____

_____

Spell Casting Details: _____

_____

_____

_____

_____

_____

_____

_____

_____

_____

_____

Spell #: _____

Spell Name: _____
_____

Spell Items: _____ _____
_____ _____ _____
_____ _____ _____
_____ _____ _____
_____ _____ _____

Preferred Moon Phase: _____

Preferred Times of Day: 06:00 07:00 08:00 09:00
10:00 11:00 12:00 13:00 14:00 15:00 16:00 17:00
18:00 19:00 20:00 21:00 22:00 23:00 24:00 _____
_____

Spell Casting Details: _____
_____
_____
_____
_____
_____
_____
_____
_____
_____

Spell #: _____

Spell Name: _____

_____

Spell Items: _____   _____

_____   _____   _____

_____   _____   _____

_____   _____   _____

_____   _____   _____

Preferred Moon Phase: _____

Preferred Times of Day: 06:00 07:00 08:00 09:00 10:00 11:00 12:00 13:00 14:00 15:00 16:00 17:00 18:00 19:00 20:00 21:00 22:00 23:00 24:00 _____

Spell Casting Details: _____

_____

_____

_____

_____

_____

_____

_____

_____

_____

_____

Spell #: _____

Spell Name: _____

_____

Spell Items: _____ _____

_____ _____

_____ _____

_____ _____

_____ _____

Preferred Moon Phase:_____

Preferred Times of Day: 06:00 07:00 08:00 09:00
10:00 11:00 12:00 13:00 14:00 15:00 16:00 17:00
18:00 19:00 20:00 21:00 22:00 23:00 24:00 _____

_____

Spell Casting Details:_____

_____

_____

_____

_____

_____

_____

_____

_____

_____

_____

Spell #: _____

Spell Name: _____

_____

Spell Items: _____   _____

_____   _____   _____

_____   _____   _____

_____   _____   _____

_____   _____   _____

Preferred Moon Phase: _____

Preferred Times of Day: 06:00 07:00 08:00 09:00
10:00 11:00 12:00 13:00 14:00 15:00 16:00 17:00
18:00 19:00 20:00 21:00 22:00 23:00 24:00 _____

Spell Casting Details: _____

_____

_____

_____

_____

_____

_____

_____

_____

_____

_____

_____

Spell #: _____

Spell Name: _____

_____

Spell Items: _____   _____

_____   _____

_____   _____

_____   _____

_____   _____

Preferred Moon Phase: _____

Preferred Times of Day: 06:00 07:00 08:00 09:00 10:00 11:00 12:00 13:00 14:00 15:00 16:00 17:00 18:00 19:00 20:00 21:00 22:00 23:00 24:00 _____

_____

Spell Casting Details: _____

_____

_____

_____

_____

_____

_____

_____

_____

_____

Spell #: _____

Spell Name: _____
_____

Spell Items: _____ _____
_____ _____ _____
_____ _____ _____
_____ _____ _____
_____ _____ _____

Preferred Moon Phase: _____

Preferred Times of Day: 06:00 07:00 08:00 09:00
10:00 11:00 12:00 13:00 14:00 15:00 16:00 17:00
18:00 19:00 20:00 21:00 22:00 23:00 24:00 _____

Spell Casting Details: _____
_____
_____
_____
_____
_____
_____
_____
_____
_____
_____

Spell #: _____

Spell Name: _____
_____

Spell Items: _____ _____
_____ _____ _____
_____ _____ _____
_____ _____ _____
_____ _____ _____

Preferred Moon Phase: _____

Preferred Times of Day: 06:00 07:00 08:00 09:00
10:00 11:00 12:00 13:00 14:00 15:00 16:00 17:00
18:00 19:00 20:00 21:00 22:00 23:00 24:00 _____
_____

Spell Casting Details: _____
_____
_____
_____
_____
_____
_____
_____
_____
_____
_____
_____

Spell #: _____

Spell Name: _____

_____

Spell Items: _____ _____

_____ _____ _____

_____ _____ _____

_____ _____ _____

_____ _____ _____

Preferred Moon Phase:_____

Preferred Times of Day: 06:00 07:00 08:00 09:00
10:00 11:00 12:00 13:00 14:00 15:00 16:00 17:00
18:00 19:00 20:00 21:00 22:00 23:00 24:00 _____

_____

Spell Casting Details:_____

_____

_____

_____

_____

_____

_____

_____

_____

_____

_____

_____

Spell #: _____

Spell Name: _____

_____

Spell Items: _____ _____

_____ _____ _____

_____ _____ _____

_____ _____ _____

_____ _____ _____

Preferred Moon Phase:_____

**Preferred Times of Day: 06:00 07:00 08:00 09:00
10:00 11:00 12:00 13:00 14:00 15:00 16:00 17:00
18:00 19:00 20:00 21:00 22:00 23:00 24:00** _____

_____

Spell Casting Details:_____

_____

_____

_____

_____

_____

_____

_____

_____

_____

_____

Spell #: _____

Spell Name: _____

_____

Spell Items: _____ _____

_____ _____ _____

_____ _____ _____

_____ _____ _____

_____ _____ _____

Preferred Moon Phase: _____

Preferred Times of Day: 06:00 07:00 08:00 09:00 10:00 11:00 12:00 13:00 14:00 15:00 16:00 17:00 18:00 19:00 20:00 21:00 22:00 23:00 24:00 _____

_____

Spell Casting Details: _____

_____

_____

_____

_____

_____

_____

_____

_____

_____

_____

Spell #: _____

Spell Name: _____

_____

Spell Items: _____ _____

_____ _____

_____ _____

_____ _____

_____ _____

Preferred Moon Phase: _____

Preferred Times of Day: 06:00 07:00 08:00 09:00
10:00 11:00 12:00 13:00 14:00 15:00 16:00 17:00
18:00 19:00 20:00 21:00 22:00 23:00 24:00 _____

_____

Spell Casting Details: _____

_____

_____

_____

_____

_____

_____

_____

_____

_____

_____

Spell #: _____

Spell Name: _____

_____

Spell Items: _____ _____

_____ _____ _____

_____ _____ _____

_____ _____ _____

_____ _____ _____

Preferred Moon Phase: _____

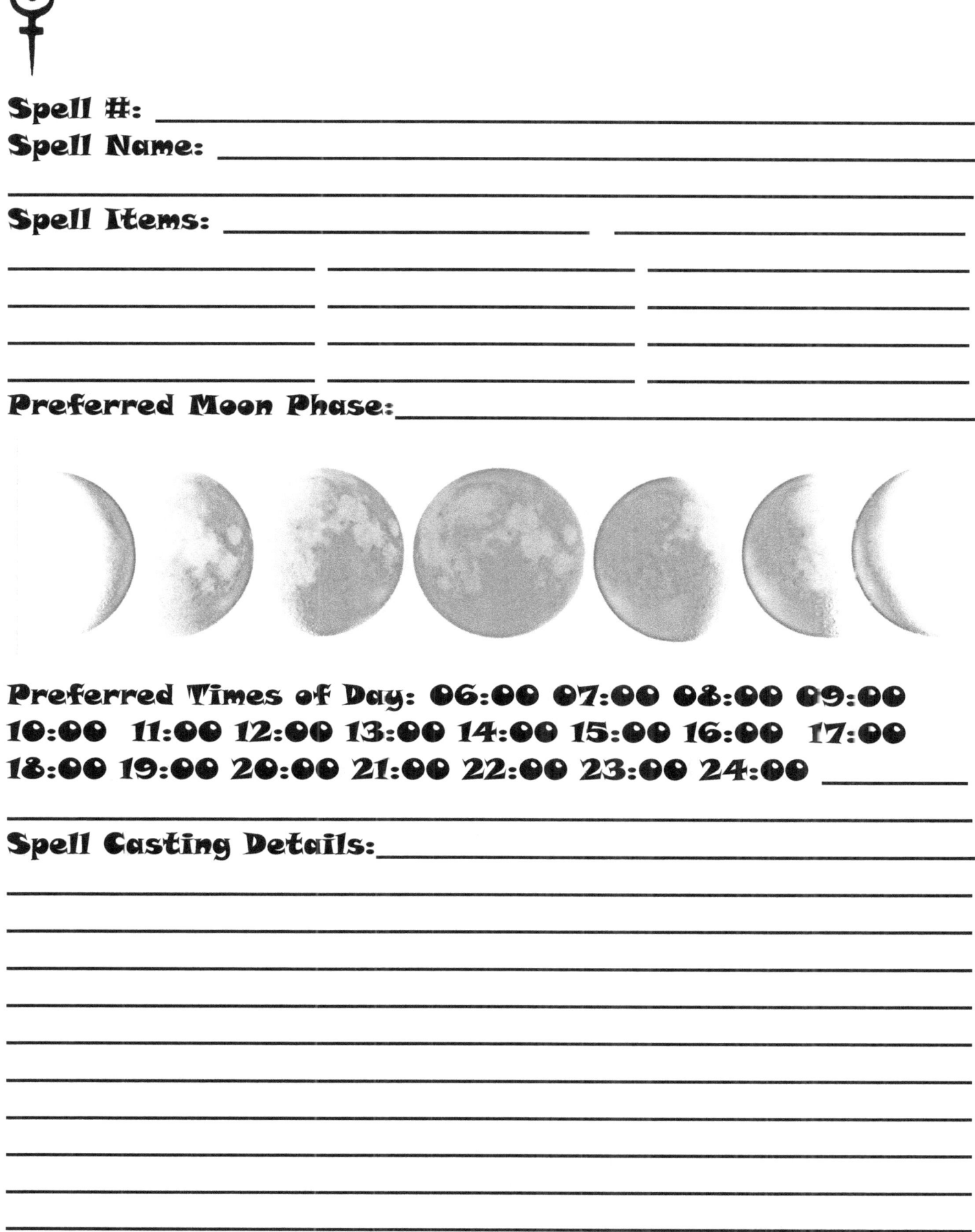

Preferred Times of Day: 06:00 07:00 08:00 09:00
10:00 11:00 12:00 13:00 14:00 15:00 16:00 17:00
18:00 19:00 20:00 21:00 22:00 23:00 24:00 _____

Spell Casting Details: _____

_____

_____

_____

_____

_____

_____

_____

_____

_____

_____

Spell #: _____

Spell Name: _____

_____

Spell Items: _____   _____

_____   _____   _____

_____   _____   _____

_____   _____   _____

_____   _____   _____

Preferred Moon Phase: _____

**Preferred Times of Day: 06:00 07:00 08:00 09:00
10:00 11:00 12:00 13:00 14:00 15:00 16:00 17:00
18:00 19:00 20:00 21:00 22:00 23:00 24:00** _____

_____

Spell Casting Details: _____

_____

_____

_____

_____

_____

_____

_____

_____

_____

_____

_____

Spell #: _____

Spell Name: _____

_____

Spell Items: _____   _____

_____   _____   _____

_____   _____   _____

_____   _____   _____

_____   _____

Preferred Moon Phase: _____

Preferred Times of Day: 06:00 07:00 08:00 09:00 10:00 11:00 12:00 13:00 14:00 15:00 16:00 17:00 18:00 19:00 20:00 21:00 22:00 23:00 24:00 _____

_____

Spell Casting Details: _____

_____

_____

_____

_____

_____

_____

_____

_____

_____

_____

Spell #: _____

Spell Name: _____

_____

Spell Items: _____ _____

_____ _____ _____

_____ _____ _____

_____ _____ _____

_____ _____ _____

Preferred Moon Phase: _____

Preferred Times of Day: 06:00 07:00 08:00 09:00 10:00 11:00 12:00 13:00 14:00 15:00 16:00 17:00 18:00 19:00 20:00 21:00 22:00 23:00 24:00 _____

_____

Spell Casting Details: _____

_____

_____

_____

_____

_____

_____

_____

_____

_____

Spell #: _____

Spell Name: _____

_____

Spell Items: _____ _____

_____ _____ _____

_____ _____ _____

_____ _____ _____

_____ _____ _____

Preferred Moon Phase:_____

**Preferred Times of Day: 06:00 07:00 08:00 09:00
10:00 11:00 12:00 13:00 14:00 15:00 16:00 17:00
18:00 19:00 20:00 21:00 22:00 23:00 24:00** _____

_____

Spell Casting Details:_____

_____

_____

_____

_____

_____

_____

_____

_____

_____

_____

_____

Spell #: _____

Spell Name: _____
_____

Spell Items: _____ _____
_____ _____ _____
_____ _____ _____
_____ _____ _____
_____ _____ _____

Preferred Moon Phase: _____

**Preferred Times of Day: 06:00 07:00 08:00 09:00
10:00 11:00 12:00 13:00 14:00 15:00 16:00 17:00
18:00 19:00 20:00 21:00 22:00 23:00 24:00** _____

Spell Casting Details: _____
_____
_____
_____
_____
_____
_____
_____
_____
_____
_____

Spell #: _____

Spell Name: _____
_____

Spell Items: _____ _____
_____ _____ _____
_____ _____ _____
_____ _____ _____
_____ _____ _____

Preferred Moon Phase: _____

Preferred Times of Day: 06:00 07:00 08:00 09:00
10:00 11:00 12:00 13:00 14:00 15:00 16:00 17:00
18:00 19:00 20:00 21:00 22:00 23:00 24:00 _____
_____

Spell Casting Details: _____
_____
_____
_____
_____
_____
_____
_____
_____
_____
_____

Spell #: _____

Spell Name: _____
_____

Spell Items: _____ _____
_____ _____ _____
_____ _____ _____
_____ _____ _____
_____ _____ _____

Preferred Moon Phase:_____

**Preferred Times of Day: 06:00 07:00 08:00 09:00
10:00 11:00 12:00 13:00 14:00 15:00 16:00 17:00
18:00 19:00 20:00 21:00 22:00 23:00 24:00 _____**
_____

Spell Casting Details:_____
_____
_____
_____
_____
_____
_____
_____
_____
_____
_____

Spell #: _____

Spell Name: _____

_____

Spell Items: _____ _____

_____ _____ _____

_____ _____ _____

_____ _____ _____

_____ _____ _____

Preferred Moon Phase:_____

Preferred Times of Day: 06:00 07:00 08:00 09:00
10:00 11:00 12:00 13:00 14:00 15:00 16:00 17:00
18:00 19:00 20:00 21:00 22:00 23:00 24:00 _____

_____

Spell Casting Details:_____

_____

_____

_____

_____

_____

_____

_____

_____

_____

_____

_____

Spell #: _____

Spell Name: _____
_____

Spell Items: _____   _____
_____   _____   _____
_____   _____   _____
_____   _____   _____
_____   _____   _____

Preferred Moon Phase:_____

**Preferred Times of Day: 06:00 07:00 08:00 09:00
10:00 11:00 12:00 13:00 14:00 15:00 16:00 17:00
18:00 19:00 20:00 21:00 22:00 23:00 24:00** _____
_____

Spell Casting Details:_____
_____
_____
_____
_____
_____
_____
_____
_____
_____
_____

Spell #: _____

Spell Name: _____

_____

Spell Items: _____   _____

_____ _____ _____

_____ _____ _____

_____ _____ _____

_____ _____ _____

Preferred Moon Phase: _____

Preferred Times of Day: 06:00 07:00 08:00 09:00
10:00 11:00 12:00 13:00 14:00 15:00 16:00 17:00
18:00 19:00 20:00 21:00 22:00 23:00 24:00 _____

Spell Casting Details: _____

_____

_____

_____

_____

_____

_____

_____

_____

_____

_____

Spell #: _____

Spell Name: _____
_____

Spell Items: _____ _____

_____ _____ _____

_____ _____ _____

_____ _____ _____

_____ _____ _____

Preferred Moon Phase: _____

Preferred Times of Day: 06:00 07:00 08:00 09:00
10:00 11:00 12:00 13:00 14:00 15:00 16:00 17:00
18:00 19:00 20:00 21:00 22:00 23:00 24:00 _____

Spell Casting Details: _____

_____

_____

_____

_____

_____

_____

_____

_____

_____

_____

Spell #: _____

Spell Name: _____
_____

Spell Items: _____ _____
_____ _____ _____
_____ _____ _____
_____ _____ _____
_____ _____ _____

Preferred Moon Phase: _____

Preferred Times of Day: 06:00 07:00 08:00 09:00
10:00 11:00 12:00 13:00 14:00 15:00 16:00 17:00
18:00 19:00 20:00 21:00 22:00 23:00 24:00 _____

Spell Casting Details: _____
_____
_____
_____
_____
_____
_____
_____
_____
_____
_____
_____

Spell #: _____

Spell Name: _____
_____

Spell Items: _____ _____
_____ _____ _____
_____ _____ _____
_____ _____ _____
_____ _____ _____

Preferred Moon Phase: _____

**Preferred Times of Day: 06:00 07:00 08:00 09:00
10:00 11:00 12:00 13:00 14:00 15:00 16:00 17:00
18:00 19:00 20:00 21:00 22:00 23:00 24:00** _____
_____

Spell Casting Details: _____
_____
_____
_____
_____
_____
_____
_____
_____
_____
_____

Spell #: _____

Spell Name: _____
_____

Spell Items: _____ _____
_____ _____ _____
_____ _____ _____
_____ _____ _____

Preferred Moon Phase: _____

Preferred Times of Day: 06:00 07:00 08:00 09:00
10:00 11:00 12:00 13:00 14:00 15:00 16:00 17:00
18:00 19:00 20:00 21:00 22:00 23:00 24:00 _____

Spell Casting Details: _____
_____
_____
_____
_____
_____
_____
_____
_____
_____
_____
_____

Spell #: _____

Spell Name: _____

_____

Spell Items: _____ _____

_____ _____ _____

_____ _____ _____

_____ _____ _____

Preferred Moon Phase:_____

Preferred Times of Day: 06:00 07:00 08:00 09:00
10:00 11:00 12:00 13:00 14:00 15:00 16:00 17:00
18:00 19:00 20:00 21:00 22:00 23:00 24:00 _____

_____

Spell Casting Details:_____

_____

_____

_____

_____

_____

_____

_____

_____

_____

Spell #: _____

Spell Name: _____

_____

Spell Items: _____ _____

_____ _____ _____

_____ _____ _____

_____ _____ _____

_____ _____ _____

Preferred Moon Phase: _____

Preferred Times of Day: 06:00 07:00 08:00 09:00
10:00 11:00 12:00 13:00 14:00 15:00 16:00 17:00
18:00 19:00 20:00 21:00 22:00 23:00 24:00 _____

Spell Casting Details: _____

_____

_____

_____

_____

_____

_____

_____

_____

_____

_____

Spell #: _____

Spell Name: _____

_____

Spell Items: _____ _____

_____ _____ _____

_____ _____ _____

_____ _____ _____

_____ _____ _____

Preferred Moon Phase:_____

Preferred Times of Day: 06:00 07:00 08:00 09:00
10:00 11:00 12:00 13:00 14:00 15:00 16:00 17:00
18:00 19:00 20:00 21:00 22:00 23:00 24:00 _____

_____

Spell Casting Details:_____

_____

_____

_____

_____

_____

_____

_____

_____

_____

_____

_____

Spell #: _____

Spell Name: _____
_____

Spell Items: _____ _____
_____ _____ _____
_____ _____ _____
_____ _____ _____

Preferred Moon Phase:_____

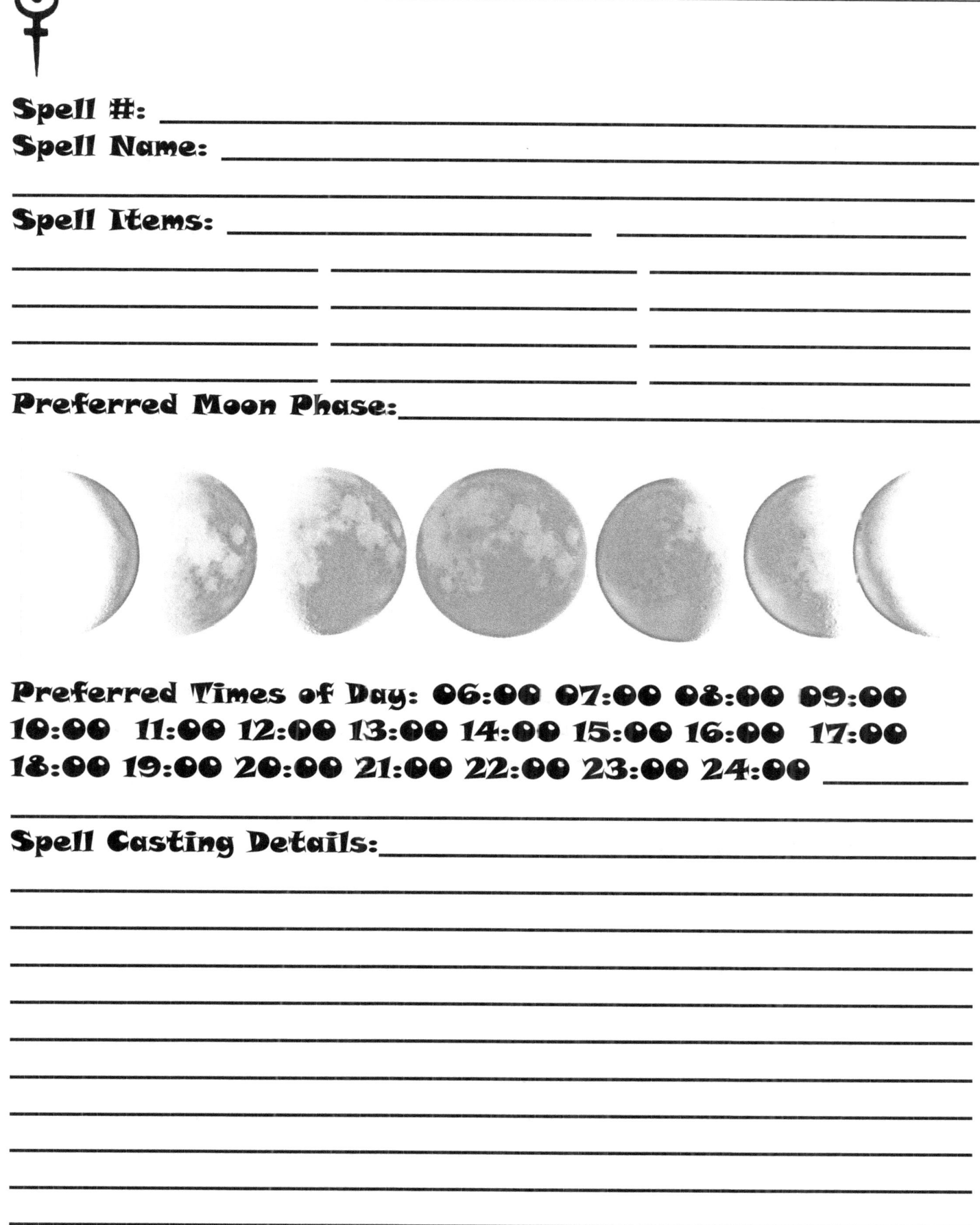

Preferred Times of Day: 06:00 07:00 08:00 09:00
10:00 11:00 12:00 13:00 14:00 15:00 16:00 17:00
18:00 19:00 20:00 21:00 22:00 23:00 24:00 _____
_____

Spell Casting Details:_____
_____
_____
_____
_____
_____
_____
_____
_____
_____
_____
_____

Spell #: _____

Spell Name: _____
_____

Spell Items: _____ _____
_____ _____ _____
_____ _____ _____
_____ _____ _____
_____ _____ _____

Preferred Moon Phase: _____

Preferred Times of Day: 06:00 07:00 08:00 09:00
10:00 11:00 12:00 13:00 14:00 15:00 16:00 17:00
18:00 19:00 20:00 21:00 22:00 23:00 24:00 _____
_____

Spell Casting Details: _____
_____
_____
_____
_____
_____
_____
_____
_____
_____
_____

Spell #: _____

Spell Name: _____

_____

Spell Items: _____ _____

_____ _____ _____

_____ _____ _____

_____ _____ _____

_____ _____ _____

Preferred Moon Phase:_____

Preferred Times of Day: 06:00 07:00 08:00 09:00
10:00 11:00 12:00 13:00 14:00 15:00 16:00 17:00
18:00 19:00 20:00 21:00 22:00 23:00 24:00 _____

_____

Spell Casting Details:_____

_____

_____

_____

_____

_____

_____

_____

_____

_____

_____

Spell #: _____

Spell Name: _____
_____

Spell Items: _____ _____

_____ _____

_____ _____

_____ _____

_____ _____

Preferred Moon Phase:_____

**Preferred Times of Day: 06:00 07:00 08:00 09:00
10:00 11:00 12:00 13:00 14:00 15:00 16:00 17:00
18:00 19:00 20:00 21:00 22:00 23:00 24:00 _____**

Spell Casting Details:_____

_____

_____

_____

_____

_____

_____

_____

_____

_____

_____

_____

Spell #: _____

Spell Name: _____

_____

Spell Items: _____ _____

_____ _____ _____

_____ _____ _____

_____ _____ _____

_____ _____ _____

Preferred Moon Phase:_____

Preferred Times of Day: 06:00 07:00 08:00 09:00
10:00 11:00 12:00 13:00 14:00 15:00 16:00 17:00
18:00 19:00 20:00 21:00 22:00 23:00 24:00 _____

Spell Casting Details:_____

_____

_____

_____

_____

_____

_____

_____

_____

_____

_____

Spell #: _____

Spell Name: _____

_____

Spell Items: _____   _____

_____   _____   _____

_____   _____   _____

_____   _____   _____

_____   _____   _____

Preferred Moon Phase: _____

Preferred Times of Day: 06:00 07:00 08:00 09:00
10:00 11:00 12:00 13:00 14:00 15:00 16:00 17:00
18:00 19:00 20:00 21:00 22:00 23:00 24:00 _____

Spell Casting Details: _____

_____

_____

_____

_____

_____

_____

_____

_____

_____

Spell #: _____

Spell Name: _____
_____

Spell Items: _____ _____

_____ _____ _____

_____ _____ _____

_____ _____ _____

_____ _____ _____

Preferred Moon Phase:_____

**Preferred Times of Day: 06:00 07:00 08:00 09:00
10:00 11:00 12:00 13:00 14:00 15:00 16:00 17:00
18:00 19:00 20:00 21:00 22:00 23:00 24:00 _____**

_____

Spell Casting Details:_____

_____

_____

_____

_____

_____

_____

_____

_____

_____

_____

Spell #: _____

Spell Name: _____

_____

Spell Items: _____ _____

_____ _____ _____

_____ _____ _____

_____ _____ _____

_____ _____ _____

Preferred Moon Phase:_____

Preferred Times of Day: 06:00 07:00 08:00 09:00 10:00 11:00 12:00 13:00 14:00 15:00 16:00 17:00 18:00 19:00 20:00 21:00 22:00 23:00 24:00 _____

_____

Spell Casting Details:_____

_____

_____

_____

_____

_____

_____

_____

_____

_____

_____

Spell #: _____

Spell Name: _____

_____

Spell Items: _____   _____

_____   _____   _____

_____   _____   _____

_____   _____   _____

_____   _____   _____

Preferred Moon Phase:_____

Preferred Times of Day: 06:00 07:00 08:00 09:00
10:00 11:00 12:00 13:00 14:00 15:00 16:00 17:00
18:00 19:00 20:00 21:00 22:00 23:00 24:00 _____

_____

Spell Casting Details:_____

_____

_____

_____

_____

_____

_____

_____

_____

_____

_____

Spell #: _____

Spell Name: _____
_____

Spell Items: _____ _____
_____ _____ _____
_____ _____ _____
_____ _____ _____
_____ _____ _____

Preferred Moon Phase:_____

Preferred Times of Day: 06:00 07:00 08:00 09:00
10:00 11:00 12:00 13:00 14:00 15:00 16:00 17:00
18:00 19:00 20:00 21:00 22:00 23:00 24:00 _____
_____

Spell Casting Details:_____
_____
_____
_____
_____
_____
_____
_____
_____
_____
_____

Spell #: _____

Spell Name: _____

_____

Spell Items: _____ _____

_____ _____

_____ _____

_____ _____

Preferred Moon Phase: _____

Preferred Times of Day: 06:00 07:00 08:00 09:00
10:00 11:00 12:00 13:00 14:00 15:00 16:00 17:00
18:00 19:00 20:00 21:00 22:00 23:00 24:00 _____

Spell Casting Details: _____

_____

_____

_____

_____

_____

_____

_____

_____

_____

_____

Spell #: _____

Spell Name: _____

_____

Spell Items: _____ _____

_____ _____ _____

_____ _____ _____

_____ _____ _____

_____ _____ _____

Preferred Moon Phase: _____

Preferred Times of Day: 06:00 07:00 08:00 09:00
10:00 11:00 12:00 13:00 14:00 15:00 16:00 17:00
18:00 19:00 20:00 21:00 22:00 23:00 24:00 _____

_____

Spell Casting Details: _____

_____

_____

_____

_____

_____

_____

_____

_____

_____

_____

Spell #: _____

Spell Name: _____

_____

Spell Items: _____ _____

_____ _____ _____

_____ _____ _____

_____ _____ _____

Preferred Moon Phase: _____

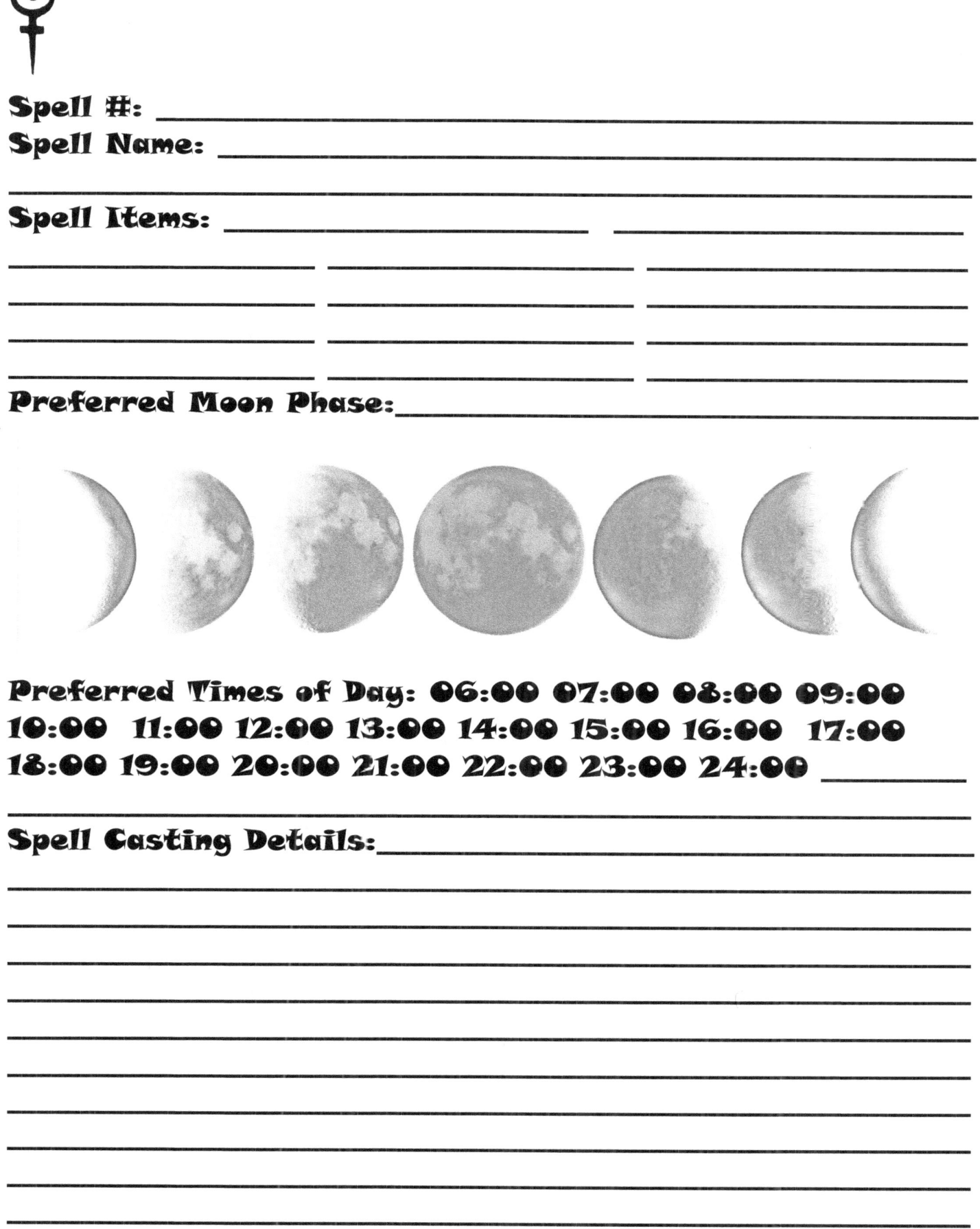

Preferred Times of Day: 06:00 07:00 08:00 09:00
10:00 11:00 12:00 13:00 14:00 15:00 16:00 17:00
18:00 19:00 20:00 21:00 22:00 23:00 24:00 _____

_____

Spell Casting Details: _____

_____

_____

_____

_____

_____

_____

_____

_____

_____

_____

General Notes:_____

General Notes:_____

General Notes:_____

General Notes:_____

General Notes:

General Notes:

General Notes:_____

General Notes:_____

General Notes:_____

General Notes:_____

General Notes:_____

General Notes:_____

_____
_____
_____
_____
_____
_____
_____
_____
_____
_____
_____
_____
_____
_____
_____
_____
_____
_____
_____
_____
_____
_____
_____
_____
_____
_____
_____